ONE BOY'S
WAR

P'

ONE BOY'S WAR

Richard Hough

Pen & Sword
AVIATION

First published in Great Britain in 1975 by William Heinemann Ltd
Reprinted in this format in 2007 by
PEN & SWORD AVIATION
an imprint of
Pen & Sword Books Ltd
47 Church Street
Barnsley
South Yorkshire
S70 2AS

ISBN 978 1 84415 690 0

A CIP catalogue record for this book is
available from the British Library

Printed and bound in Great Britain
by CPI UK

Pen & Sword Books Ltd incorporates the imprints of
Pen & Sword Aviation, Pen & Sword Maritime, Pen & Sword Military,
Wharncliffe Local History, Pen & Sword Select,
Pen & Sword Military Classics and Leo Cooper.

For a complete list of Pen & Sword titles please contact
PEN & SWORD BOOKS LIMITED
47 Church Street, Barnsley, South Yorkshire, S70 2AS, England
E-mail: enquiries@pen-and-sword.co.uk
Website: www.pen-and-sword.co.uk

FOR ROLAND GANT
who fell out of them

A small part of the early chapters appeared in the London *Evening Standard* in a different form.

When it seemed appropriate, I have changed the names of some of the R.A.F. people.

I took most of the photographs myself. I recently gave the copyright and all the negatives of my R.A.F. photographs to the Imperial War Museum. They are reproduced here by kind permission of the Trustees.

Illustrations

1a Stearman Primary Trainer, North American Harvard Advance Trainers, and Vultee Basic Trainers, 1941.

1b Night flying outside Hollywood.

2a Rare cloud over the Sierra Nevada.

2b Formation flying and photographing at the same time. Camera and film were a present from Joan Fontaine.

3ab Herbert Marshall and Nigel Bruce, Hollywood 1941.

3c The shaded home of Ronald Colman, Hollywood 1941.

4a Ronald Colman with Joan Fontaine, Mrs Charles Boyer and Brian Aherne.

4b The Brian Aherne–Joan Fontaine bar.

5 Joan Fontaine had just won her Oscar for her lead in *Suspicion* with Cary Grant.

6a Brian Aherne about to take the plunge, with his sister-in-law Olivia de Havilland, and friend.

6b Cadet Hough, in borrowed tennis gear, about to take to the court.

vii

6c   Heather Angel.

7ab Hangover dawn at Ludham after an eventful 21st birthday party.

7c   Typhoon 1b at Coltishall. H for Harry saw me safely through the busy Autumn of 1943 but was herself a bit knocked about.

8a   Rocket Tiffy.

8b   Honeymoon break in the Lake District, July 1943.

9   Flak over a convoy off the Dutch.

10ab Landing after hectic Rhine crossing operations, March 1945.

11   A scruffy Flight Lieutenant in April 1945 armed with two 500 pounders, four 20mm cannon and a .38 Smith & Wesson.

Inset, our first daughter's first birthday.

12a Parachute Brigade H.Q. near Oldenburg after 197 Squadron had dealt with it with 500 pounder delayed action bombs. I went back and took this a few hours later.

12b German ground fire remained lethal right to the end of the war. Fellow pilot is Bobby Farmiloe.

13ab Military store near Oldenburg dive-bombed by 197 Squadron with 500 pounders.

14   Forward airstrip Mill, Holland, February 1945.

15a With 24 cylinders, sleeve valves, 2-stage supercharger, and two and a half thousand horsepower, the Tiffy's Sabre engine was a fitter's nightmare.

15b Re-arming with 20mm cannon shells after a straffing raid.

16ab Sharing airfields with our old protagonists like the Heinkel 219 and the long-nose Focke-Wulf 190 and Messerschmitt Me 110.

1

Lovely Ginger Rogers rested her chin in the palms of her pretty little hands and looked up at me with her soft eyes. She was sucking through a straw from an immensely complicated drink, a super-super icecream soda topped with fruit. She drank from it with the compulsion of an alcoholic, disengaged the straw and said, 'Tell me about flying?'

'Ah!' I replied, and told her. I told her of loops and Immelmanns, spins and rolls, and hinted modestly at my dexterity with the joystick. In glamorous Hollywood in 1941 who was to know that the wings standing out boldly on my shoulders were not the real thing? There was a propeller at the top of my sleeves—the mark of a leading aircraftsman, no less—as if to confirm that I was an indomitable hero of the Battle of Britain.

The fairy-tale world of Hollywood was the right setting for shooting a line, and especially this fantasy bar in Ginger's fantasy castle. Behind her there reared up like a golden Würlitzer the machinery for mixing her concoctions. Beneath it on a shelf were the many-coloured jars and bottles of flavours, an icecream dispenser and an ice-making machine. Nearer to hand, to which Ginger often stretched one for a grape, was a colossal cornucopia of fresh fruit.

'. . . and to spin off the top,' continued 1941's very own Captain Ball, V.C., 'you ease the stick. . . . Ginger smiled a tired smile. Of course it was tired. The Fred Astaire pictures, Joan Fontaine had told me, had almost killed her. Dancing, dancing, dancing. And she had just finished another picture. Eight pages of *Life* magazine were given up to it that very week.

This was her bar, her icecream soda bar, her dream since childhood. You were invited to Ginger's castle, her mansion up in airy Bel Air above Beverly Hills, for tea not cocktails. But as a reluctant concession to boozers there was a bar at the other end of the room. It was well equipped, and more orthodoxly equipped, too. Behind it Brian Ahearne was at that moment playing host to Ronald Colman, Maureen O'Hara, C. Aubrey Smith, Basil Rathbone, Nigel Bruce, Joan Bennett, Joan Fontaine, her sister beautiful Olivia de Havilland, and other golden stars of Kinemaland. And Artur Rubinstein for good measure, and for playing the piano.

But there was someone else my keen airman's eyes should not have missed. Like Baron von Richthofen diving from out of the sun, another figure was coming up from astern, thumb, so to speak, hovering over the gun button.

I continued my graphic account innocently unaware. '. . . and of course you often black out when you pull up from a steep dive. . . .'

Then I saw in the half light Ginger's eyes shift from mine to some point behind and above me. 'Hullo!' she said, her voice on a rising note of affection.

'Ginger!' It was a deep voice, manly, authoritative.

I turned on my stool, and there at point-blank range stood a tall, formidable figure, chest emblazoned with *real* wings and a kaleidoscope of medal ribbons. I came to earth with a bumpy landing, and Ginger Rogers asked naïvely, 'Do you know Wing Commander Stanford-Tuck?'

'No,' I gulped, then leapt to my feet, remembering his rank and all those Huns he had downed in the Battle of Britain. 'No, *Sir*.'

He did not know me either, and quite right, too. If he had

2

acknowledged my existence it could only be to ask what this imitation airman was doing here at all, with *his* Ginger—this erk who had never seen a Messerschmitt, nor so much as baled out over the white cliffs of Dover.

I slunk away in search of cloud cover like a shattered Dornier. Fortunately the patrons of the boozy end of the bar were in splendid form. Within a dozen paces I had passed from the tinsel fairyland of glam movieland and was soon enmeshed in what might have been the Spider's Web on the Watford by-pass.

Nigel Bruce withdrew his pipe, took a good swallow of bitter, and asked in his husky voice, 'What about a round of golf tomorrow, old boy?'

'Good show,' remarked C. Aubrey Smith, giving his grey moustache a stroke. 'And he's promised to play cricket next week-end.'

'Magnifique!' commented Charles Boyer. French cricket? I mused.

Joan Bennett slipped me a bloody mary and came up comfortingly close, too. Her voice was even huskier. 'Are you having fun?'

I nodded. And once again there stole over me the sense of being suspended above a desert of disbelief—rather like my first solo of a few weeks before in that antiquated stringbag the Americans insisted on calling a 'ship'.

What *was* I doing here? I asked myself yet again as the tomato juice and hot vodka slipped down my young and innocent throat.

It had all been very nasty indeed at first. I was as uncertain why I had volunteered at all as I was later to wonder at the strange course of fate that was to despatch me from bombed, gallant little England to my first campaign in sun-drenched, exciting Hollywood.

At school I was bedevilled by doubts. We all were except the maths master who was considered very old-fashioned to be

3

firm in his beliefs, and an Italian who taught French and was an anarchist. We tended to despise the first for his firm convictions, though he was a good teacher and held the school together, and frankly admired the second, who gave us cigarettes, told very racy stories, but was confined to a camp in the Isle of Man soon after war broke out. He was, however, let out as a hero the moment Jo Stalin became all the rage.

These doubts were vaguely pacifist. Franco was bad and must be stopped. Hitler was bad and should not have invaded Austria and Czechoslovakia like that. Nor should he have been cruel to the Jews. We knew all about that because we had a number of German and Austrian Jewish boys who had seen their fathers beaten and made to scrub the pavement.

But war was worse than Hitler. Russia, being left, was good, at least until her pact with Hitler, and then Finland—those splendid Finns in their snowshoes—became gallant and the subject of Russia rather faded from our pronouncements.

An invasion of England would be bad, of course, but the senior boys in a body refused the ancient rifles thrust at them to shoot German parachute troops from the school bell tower, which to the shame of our maths master had to be manned by Local Defence Volunteers. But it was all right, because it was pacific I suppose, to help with an enormous anti-tank ditch which was dug for a short distance and with no apparent tactical function alongside the new local by-pass road.

We were all pathetically woolly, but I would not want to mock entirely our ideas which were sort of fumblingly well intentioned. In my case the confusion was further compounded by a strictly pacifist homelife, all muddled up my own obsessive enthusiasm for warships and navies. I knew every statistic in *Jane's Fighting Ships* by heart at 13, lectured a rather glum school audience about the history of the battleship at 14 and followed every naval bombing and bombardment in the Spanish Civil War with what others regarded as eccentric enthusiasm.

I had even, quite recently, tried to get into Dartmouth Naval College. My father was so dismayed at the idea of having a naval officer for a son that he chose a minute German cargo ship to take me across the North Sea in a full gale just to show I was not made for the life. As I was conscious for only the first three hours I suppose he was right, although I reflected later that he was a bit muddled, too, being an avowed Bolshevik and also a Brighton bank manager for Barclays.

A boy called Martin Rivers came to teach gym at our school. He had been at Bedales, another co-ed place well known for doubts, unorthodoxy, rather long shorts and open-neck Aertex shirts. He was 6 feet 4 or so and crashingly handsome. Most of the senior girls and women staff fell head over heels in love with him before half term. All the boys admired him, of course, and when he made it abundantly clear that he was a pacifist, too, we all became even more so.

We were truly sorry about the invasion of Norway and we were sorry about the fall of France, too, and I think at Dunkirk we rather caught our breaths and began to wonder about the realities of pacifism. But I was head boy during that grave business, very full of school and athletics records and being passionately in love with a girl called Charlotte.

But when Martin Rivers changed his mind, so did we. It was horrible, but Hitler, it seemed, had to be stopped. We felt no arousal of bloodthirstiness. Our feelings were ones of mournful acceptance of the inevitability of having to fight, tinged with a certain self-conscious fastidiousness about the business; superior because we were really above such things, ashamed because we were compromising our convictions.

Some of the senior boys and young staff put on uniform but drove ambulances only, or dug in those regiments that dig behind the front line. One boy destined for the D-Day landing four years later changed his mind on about D minus 5 and reverted to pacifism, which must have taken some doing.

The turning point at our school was not so much the gallant

overcoming of the Luftwaffe in the Battle of Britain but the overturning of Martin Rivers's convictions. And, by golly, if Martin Rivers was going aloft with the boys in blue, I would be there with him.

In fact, it took rather a long time because, first I was too young, then you had to wait for medical examinations and goodness knows what.

So I did some teaching at a rum sort of prep. school run by several Captain Grimeses without a qualification between them, and did some ambulance driving near Charlotte, finding home life at Brighton a bit drab at that time and myself sadly out of harmony with my father who gave the impression he didn't want me to fight *or* be a pacifist.

By June 1941, when the R.A.F. at last claimed me for its own, Martin Rivers had already been killed in a Hurricane. Charlotte and I became informally engaged, with the understanding that we would marry after the war—off to which I went with a high heart.

Those first days would have been perfectly bearable if I had not so far led such a protected life, without even the rigours and competition of an orthodox boys' public school. Everyone had been so kind and understanding at school while scattering their seeds of liberal questioning and goodwill. Watered by the early distresses and discomforts of service life, the doubts began to sprout again. Even if I ever got as far as the cockpit of a Hurricane, I feared my finger would hesitate fatally on that gun button.

I was just nineteen, very unsure, fearful of the real world, and in spite of a supposedly liberated education, rather prudish. To my utter shame, the whole experience became too much for me and I was plotting desertion before I even got my uniform. Hardly Captain Ball stuff.

In a once rather elegant corner of Regent's Park in north-west London an obnoxious form of animal life appeared in 1941.

6

They were called aircrew cadets and they lived like weevils in a long line of ex-luxury flats overlooking the canal, with windows bricked up (a brick missing for ventilation) and bells outside to warn of gas attacks. There was Bentinck Close and Viceroy Court and St James's Close. Today I suppose a lease changes hands at around £100,000. In 1941 we were paid two bob a day to live there, five to a room.

It was a constantly changing population of 2,500 or so, herded about by ferocious non-commissioned officers, backed up by R.A.F. police, to be sorted out and kitted.

I found it exceedingly difficult to reconcile these beings who might have come from another planet, who cursed in many incomprehensible dialects and were of so many different shapes and sizes, with our gallant boys in blue, the *crème de la crème* —pilots of the Royal Air Force.

For three weeks, and in Flights (Ha!) of fifty, we plunged about the streets of St John's Wood at first in the disarray of civilian clothes, and then in coarse stiff new uniforms, boots styled for the Crimean War, blanco-ed belts and forage caps with a white flash in the peak to confirm our lowly status.

There was a busy and memorable morning in the sacred members' pavilion at Lords where, beneath the bearded, scowling figure of W. G. Grace and other great cricketers of the past, we were punctured in the chest and arms with every sort of vaccine, and tested for venereal disease and told to cough while someone clung on to our testicles. It was a levelling experience—in two ways, really, as a large number of the white and not always well-shaped bodies fell flat with shock to the floor and were carried off by orderlies, just as if this was an exercise in genocide, which it nearly was.

Uniforms and equipment of some complexity were hurled at us by veteran tailors who measured us by eye as we marched into a requisitioned garage and turned to the stacks behind them and in one co-ordinated movement directed at us basic trousers and jacket, two shirts, knee-length woolly pants, vests;

7

then, with a second swing, boots and socks. The range of exotica included mysteries like button sticks and anti-gas ointment. In the end the kitbag weighed over a hundredweight as we staggered out into the drizzle and went back to our dark rooms to wrap up in old brown paper the last vestiges of our old selves to post home.

Meals were taken, appropriately, in the Zoo. The members' dining-rooms had been taken over, stripped, and equipped with long benches. It could take two hours to fight your way in. Bogey was ninety minutes. At one breakfast I counted seven figures slumped on the forms, heads in their dishes, unconscious from exhaustion after the long struggle to get in. The smells from the cooking vats blended with those from the caged animals, notably from the mountain goats. On the way out you dipped your eating irons into a bucket of tepid water with a many-coloured skin of grease on the surface—all ready for the next chap.

In the evenings we were allowed out within a short radius, too short for me to reach legally Charlotte's home at Bushey. But, desperately daring, I would tear the tell-tale white flash from my cap and hitch-hike out north for an hour of home comforts and outpourings of my woes. Then back to the dark corridors and sour-smelling rooms of the flats where obscenities accompanied tales of illicit copulation in the parks, and the heavy new boots beat on naked floors and stairs. (No electricity for lifts or lights, of course.)

The St John's Wood experience was but one stage in the R.A.F.'s blunt processing procedure which worked on the basis of accepting almost anything that walked at this bravely named Air Crew Receiving Centre, and then sifting ruthlessly. I suppose just removing all who fainted from shock or starvation was a start, if an unrefined one. Fifteen-minute pre-selection intelligence tests, as they were euphemistically called, got rid of a few more. Word among the permanent veterans at A.C.R.C. had it that only 13% ever saw the inside of an aeroplane though

I imagine this was raised a good deal when the Germans began to decimate the bomber crews later.

After all that, the luxury of Babbacombe on the Devonshire Riviera was almost overwhelming. The howls of Spitfires and Hurricanes, the rattle of multiple Browning .303s, silk scarves billowing in the slipstream, the victory rolls, the thin trickle of blood from the corner of the Hun's mouth as he goes down in flames—all that sort of thing was still as remote as Captain Ball in my dreams. But here we were called a Wing—if only an Initial Training one—and we did see aeroplanes, if only in model form hanging by string. Aircraft Identification was a very serious and important subject, we were told. Soon we could spot a Heinkel 111 from a fleeting glimpse of a rudder.

Wireless and navigation seemed sensible subjects too. Morse by Aldis lamp was more puzzling. Did one stand up in the cockpit at night, coming in to land, and flash for permission— 'Shot through and through like a colander—must pancake'? Stripping down and putting together again a machine-gun blindfold summoned heroic images, too—images of repairing your weapon in the heat of combat, blinded by Spandau fire, game to the end. . . .

But soon we could at least dress for the part. I was delighted to see that our flying clobber was still designed for tailing Albatros Scouts behind the Boche lines at sixteen thou.—silk gloves, woollen gloves, huge leather gauntlets over the lot; three thicknesses of flying suits, too, including an eiderdown shaped roughly to human form and an outer skin with fur collar (like the silk scarf, not for warmth but to protect the neck while twisting it to search the sky for the Red Baron) and zip pockets; two thicknesses of helmet, furlined boots, and most prized of all, goggles. Goggles spelled Biggles, and Biggles spelled Hero of the Skies.

At Babbacombe they really got us fit for the killing, and the thinning out process continued apace. It was a twelve-hour day for seven days a week for eight weeks, with little time off, and we got hard and muscular and brown in the summer sun doing exercises in the public parks and route marches for miles. Schoolboys mocked us. Retired generals (and there were plenty here) regarded us with mixed feelings, for brave lads though we might be, there was, in their eyes, something a touch raffish about the R.A.F.

There was a lot of fighting in the evenings, most of it not serious, and a certain amount of boozing. My first introduction to gin, and first experience of being paralytically drunk, took place ingloriously. But I felt marvellous at the end of the course, and my spirits, too, were better though still very mercurial. It was the only time that the Air Force paid the least attention to our fitness.

As training advanced later we got more and more physically slack, until eventually on a squadron I can remember taking no exercise at all, except occasionally heaving out of a deck chair and stumbling out to an aeroplane in an emergency—'scramble' was the unlikely word for this procedure.

Service life was built on rumours—rumours sensational, rumours false, rumours true (but rarely), rumours baleful and benign. They played a large part in civil life in the war; they dominated service life. In the R.A.F., with its penchant for slang, they were called 'gen', short for intelligence. There was 'ace gen' which sometimes bore some relation to the truth, and just ordinary 'gen' which was always false, or 'duff gen' which hardly pretended to bear any relation to the truth.

Gen of one sort or another filled the air daily among the parks with their bandstands, the genteel streets, the clifftop walks, of Babbacombe and nearby Torquay. We were to be trained in England, in South Africa, in Canada, in (surely the duffest of duff gen) the U.S.A. Our course was being lengthened, shortened, there would be leave, long leave, no leave.

So frenetically did the rumours fly, so wrought up did we become, that one valiant cadet volunteered to break into the

C.O.'s office at night and search through the papers. He returned with proof positive that we were all leaving in forty-eight hours for foreign parts, without leave. Three weeks later we were still in Babbacombe, banging away at clay pigeons, pulling rifles to bits, parading a dozen times a day, poking about in ancient aero engines.

When we did at last go in early October, it was all done in the best traditions of the wartime services. Slow, circuitous and hesitant railway journeys, by day and by night, in Edwardian rolling stock. Extemporised meals laid on by kindly volunteer ladies at wayside halts. Boredom and heat and the stench of cheap cigarettes and unwashed bodies. And tumbling out at 3 a.m. in the rain and blackout in a suburb of Manchester, hundreds and hundreds of us, and the long march to a barbed-wire-enclosed transit camp of Nissen huts.

Nothing I have experienced can match the melancholy of a wartime transit camp, with its futile time-wasting fatigues, its mindless little restrictions, half-hearted orders soon half-heartedly countermanded, the bunk blankets stiff with the dirt of transient airmen, and the rootlessness of everyone and everything. 'It comes as a nasty shock to hear a laugh here,' I wrote dismally to Charlotte in my last letter from England, begging her to marry me when I got back.

Equipment and kit were issued to us and almost at once withdrawn—tropical kit then semi-Polar kit and finally and most bizarre of all, a decidedly *démodé* civilian outfit, for all the world as if we had joined the secret service rather than the R.A.F.—fibre suitcase as used by third division football teams for away matches, double-breasted flannel suit, George Raft-style trilby hat *and* a beret (for some shabby double role?), rather co-respondentish shoes, a Woolworth tie and a very long belted overcoat.

All this sort of nonsense kept us semi-occupied during the day. We were allowed out into the dark wet streets briefly in the evenings. If the two cinemas were full—and they always were—there was nothing to do but drink warm beer, smoke cigarettes or mooch about.

At 3 a.m. on 14 October 1941 we trailed out of this camp with our suitcases and kitbags and walked a long way to a dark siding where we dropped into exhausted sleep in a troop train. The dawn awakening was agonisingly evocative for me. The train was approaching the eastern hills of the Lake District, a corner of England where I had enjoyed carefree holidays for year after year when I had been a boy, and the rolling fells, the ghylls and rowan trees and Herdwick sheep and dry-stone walls had for long represented freedom in my mind.

The train laboured up Shap at no more than fast walking pace, and I was the only one awake. It would be so easy to open the door of this prison and walk out, and I could live rough for months among these fells which I knew so well. . . . Then the train reached the summit and gathered pace down the long descent to Carlisle. Clickety-click, clickety-click back to prison. . . .

What on earth was I thinking? It was all a great big adventure, wasn't it? And surely you can't be homesick at nineteen! I just wished that there was one other person I could talk to—one would do. The rough braking of the train at the bottom of Shap woke up most of the others in my compartment. Each in turn swore, groaned, stretched and drew a battered cigarette from his tunic pocket.

The *Louis Pasteur* had been towed from its shipyard as France fell. With a displacement of 33,000 tons and a maximum speed of 35 knots, she was designed to wrest from Britain the Blue Riband of the Atlantic and acquire all the prestige of a businessman's express to the New World. But like the republic that had produced it, her life had not been a happy one since she had been launched. Her completion had been delayed by strikes and when the German armies fell on France in May 1940 she had not yet been fitted out.

Rumour had it that the *Pasteur* had a kink in her keel, the result of sabotage by twisted communist shipworkers. This caused incurable corkscrewing and she was unloved among the fighting men of the Empire. Wartime censorship had failed to stamp out reports that first Canadian and then New Zealand airmen had refused to sail in her because of the conditions on board. Now, in October 1941, British airmen were to be put to the test. Did they have the guts? Would they survive it?

I am proud to say that they did, while feeling bound to add that it was touch and go. Nobody ever recorded how many of us were eventually battened down in the flagship-to-be of the French passenger fleet. It must have been several thousand. On my mess deck the hammocks nudged one another at the mildest corkscrew and grazed the bodies of those bunking on the mess tables below. And that wasn't all. Below the mess tables and lying on the naked deck was another layer. They were the know-all boys, the lads who always got the ace gen. Down there you were beneath the worst of the stench and no one ever hit you. All right for non-claustrophobes. For me I chose the hammocks.

For three days we rode at anchor in the Clyde, and on the fourth we sailed and at the same time discovered that we were not alone. Someone penetrated the deepest bowels of the *Pasteur* and found regiments of Canadian soldiers living under cramped and such unspeakably filthy conditions that we temporarily forgot our complaints. They had not mutinied because they were on their way home—discharged for compassionate or medical reasons. They were not refined in their seasickness, we later discovered, but in quieter weather were known to emerge to fleece the gullible R.A.F. cadets above them at poker, pontoon or brag.

Among the élite on board were battle-scarred veterans of Britain's early campaigns, off to lecture in the United States and teach them a thing or two for the time when they might be in the front line. The Australian, Hughie Edwards, told us 'it was

13

just an ordinary op.' on which he had got his V.C., which sounded encouraging for us, and a Battle of Britain pilot was more explicit: 'So I squirted the gun crew and I got great joy and satisfaction seeing them fall every way'—which shocked to the core my so recently pacifist heart.

This élite, this brass, occupied half the luxury suites on the upper deck, the other half remaining bolted, to our chagrin. The lavatories were firmly bolted too, while we resorted to continuous troughs with a stripped pine tree trunk to sit upon knee by knee with our comrades—for we had not yet been 'admitted to that equal sky'. Would I ever, I wondered, as the excreta flowed to and fro with the roll of the ship?

It was very very rough and I took refuge in a deck cargo of potatoes and fell into unconsciousness for two days and nights. When I came round our escorting destroyers were still dipping out of sight to their mastheads, and even the 15-inch-gunned battleship that guarded our stern dug deeply into the autumn seas. There was nothing to do, there was no discipline and we wore what we liked as we played cards for money none of us possessed for hour after hour, looking terrible in our week-old beards.

Late one afternoon our escort deserted us, and the *Louis Pasteur* showed her true pace and we vibrated our way at over 30 knots towards Halifax where we docked on the evening of 25 October.

Now to the New World of glittering efficiency. The Canadians would show us how things were done. The lights shone brightly, cars with headlamps ablaze—when had we last seen that?—swooshed silently through the streets, and an immense train took us panting through forests and fairy-tale log cabin villages that could only be Canadian, to a sizeable township called Moncton. Here we piled out at 3 a.m. with our kitbags onto the line and began to march off through thick snow into the forest.

No one was quite sure where we should be going but we had

14

utter trust in Canadian efficiency and hospitality. We had been told that there was no welcome like a Canadian welcome, our friends in peace, our allies in war. Very wet and cold, three-quarters of an hour later, we heard the faint sounds of hammering and the calling of many deep voices in the darkness. We stumbled into a patch of light, and also into one of those traditional fairy-tales in which an army of gnomes builds a fairy queen's palace overnight. Ahead of us was a scene of controlled chaos and industry the like of which I had never seen.

Arc-lit in the night, a township was going up before our very eyes—a township of wooden huts in rows, of a main street and what might have been municipal buildings. The fronts of the half-completed buildings looked like façades, and as I got nearer the fairy-tale effect faded and the scene was more of studio workers hurrying a movie Western set to completion before the star arrived.

But we, the cast of thousands, were already there, and well before our time. The great new Royal Canadian Air Force Transit Camp at Moncton was not yet ready for its guests. It was unsettling for the site manager to see this long column of airmen emerging wearily from the darkness and snow knowing that there were no drains, no water, and in many cases no roofs for the band of brave boys in blue. It was unsettling for us, too.

So we were given blankets and buckets and told to fend for ourselves. A scratch meal would be ready some time in a partly roofless mess hall. Otherwise it was suggested that we should use the woods and eat in the town's drugstores.

The kind people of Moncton rose marvellously to the occasion, inviting us to their houses, while the drugstores and restaurants did a year's trade in three days. Some of us slept in houses, others curled up in the half-finished huts as close as possible to one of the log stoves that the workmen had got going for us.

The third day was a fateful one for all of us. The word got round that we should gather on the muddy clearance that would one day be a parade ground, with our kit. With remarkable efficiency, the Canadians had organised our distribution about the North American continent by train in 72 hours.

There was a certain amount of shouting, but by being decisive about it one or two officers arbitrarily cut out the large majority of the cadets, split them into batches of fifty and gave them destinations which sounded like Long Hoof, Saskatchewan. And off they plodded, amid jeers.

Jeers, because we, who were left behind, were suddenly aware—ace gen it was, too, not at all duff—that we were off to the good old U.S.A. where the girls were beautiful, the steaks were thick and they didn't even have a war. Three hundred we were, and continuing the slicing like relentless butchers the officers divided us into six batches of fifty—'You lot, Texas for you—you go to Florida, here are the papers and here's your itinerary, now get off to the train—Oklahoma for you . . .' and so on.

A very green pilot officer approached us holding a file. He nominated a commander at a glance and thrust the papers into his hand. We broke what ranks were left and crowded around our new pack leader. The lettering on the cover of the file was uncompromisingly clear: CALIFORNIA. And beneath this fantasy title: 'Polaris Flight Academy, Number Two British Flying School, Lancaster, California'.

What better than an Academy for learning to fly? A Flight Academy, that rang true. And a Polaris one, too. *Jolly* good show!

'Where's Lancaster, sir?' a young cadet cried.

'In a valley just outside Los Angeles.'

'What about Hollywood?'

We were told it was believed to be an easy hitch-hike away. That it was a relaxed sort of Academy, so our officer believed, that it was civilian run. 'And that's lucky for you. The ones belonging to the Army Air Corps are run like West Point and the few survivors are never the same men again.'

So it was to be war in Hollywood. There were worse places, I supposed, to fight your first campaign.

Like all wartime journeys this one, too, had its ups and downs. We travelled first-class luxury in the trains with deep reclining and swivelling seats, an observation car for observing from and a club coach for spitting, smoking and gambling in. We had a nasty evening in Montreal where the French Canadians booed and spat at us and several of us were thrown out of bars. We didn't understand that at all, being quite unaware of the deep passions that flowed in that part of Canada.

Then for neutrality reasons we had to get out our natty suitings and wide-brimmed trilbys for crossing the frontier. In the clear light of day we looked very odd indeed, some trousers revealing calves, others swallowing half the shoe. Mine, someone remarked, had been tailored for Fats Waller but I so loved that man that I felt honoured.

However, this E. Phillips Oppenheim touch only enflamed the ardour of our first Americans on the U.S. side of the town of London (home from home) at the frontier. Reporters swarmed about us and flashed away with their cameras while ladies from local ladies' clubs purred and offered coffee—'Aw, gee, we think you are all just wunnerful . . .' We felt it right then, too, as we launched into graphic accounts of the blitz and starvation to our trapped and enchanted audience.

But, we were soon asking ourselves, were we wanted or were we not? Were we among friends or enemies? En route to Chicago the word went round that we could revert to our uniforms, and proudly we did so, polishing our buttons and boots for the Windy City. Heads high, we left the station in close formation at 8 p.m. on 30 October. 'Tally ho!' someone cried, and we broke up and scattered to search for our quarries.

In bars and restaurants we answered the inevitable question with, 'Oh, it's the uniform of the R.A.F.' Sometimes this evinced surprise before hostility, but more often it was immediate hostility, and in several Irish bars the throwers-out were busy.

We were, unknowingly, in the heart of Britain-hating Hearstland and no one around here was on our side—or if they were we saw none. We re-embarked before our time, several of us again with sore heads. Was it not enough that we stood alone against the Hun? Was it to be the Yank, too? Another Battle of Bunker Hill?

In fact, that was the last of the hostility, and at every other city at which we stopped, and especially Salt Lake City, we were welcomed, in or out of uniform. So by the time we slipped into Los Angeles four days later, full of fine food and drink, we were ready to return the embrace of every loving housewife and businessman (to say nothing of their super wizzo bang-on ace girls) who met us at the station and gave us hospitality cards with their names and addresses for week-ends and leaves.

Then up we climbed into a snorting old Wild West train this time and banged and rattled our way out to the good old Antelope Valley and the Polaris Flight Academy, that mecca of future Captain Balls.

With us now in the train was a boy from that very establishment, with a flash in his cap like us but looking very blasé and time-got-in. He was a British cadet who had *soloed* no less, and he was full of ace gen which he patronisingly cast around to us new sprogs. 'That lot!' he proclaimed with scorn, nodding towards the eager waving figures on the platform as we pulled out. 'You don't want to bother with *them* with movie stars at two a dime round here. You wait,' he added knowingly, 'you'll see.'

And he curled up with a fag and a movie mag.

2

Life assumed what can only be described as a new hue in late October 1941. From war-torn, austere, rationed, blacked-out Britain, here we suddenly were in sun-drenched California, 3,000 feet up. We were also in a valley, the Antelope Valley, colourful with flowers, spectacular with giant cacti. At night the coyotes howled in protest against the moan of the transcontinental express trains and John Wayne lurked at the corner of every bar in every hick township.

Along the roadside Mexican peasants offered as much orange juice as you could drink for 5 cents, squeezed for you on the spot. Ranches hired out horses for a few bucks a day. Far in the distance but crystal clear in this air there soared the snow-clad Sierra Nevada.

Seventy miles away, beyond a ridge of hills, lay the fairy-tale world of Los Angeles, Beverly Hills and Hollywood itself. At night the glow lit up the whole southern horizon like a permanent invitation to an open-air party. Sometimes searchlights stabbed the sky, their beams probing and crossing in frantic patterns. Three weeks ago we had watched beams like these over Manchester searching for Heinkels and Dorniers. The local variety in Hollywood were celebrating another night, the première of *The Birth of the Blues* starring Bing Crosby, Louis Armstrong *et al. . . .*

At the Polaris Flight Academy we were always within the sound of aero engines, as we should have been, testing on the ground or flying overhead. But they brought us no nearer to the reality of war. There was not a gun anywhere, nor a hint of combat. We might have been Sir Alan Cobham's Flying Circus working up to a new season's entertainment, perhaps with lovely girls at the wingtips, one hand holding a strut, the other waving to the cheering crowds below.

We lived in brand new four-room-and-bath chalets arranged around lawns and gardens. Larger chalets provided lecture halls, recreation rooms, and most sumptuous of all, the dining hall. We goggled in disbelief at this on our first morning after we awoke, purged in body and soul by the crisp desert air. I was directed to it by a tough, fair-haired veteran cadet called Johnny Baldwin who had almost completed his course. 'What's the food like?' I asked. 'Not bad. Gets a bit boring.'

Boring? I stared down the length of the dining hall. Behind a line of shining hot plates, cookers and tables stood a team of chefs, white hats bobbing as they tossed wheatcakes, broke open eggs single-handed with electric speed, scooped up sizzling strips of bacon. Their wisecracks were as fast as their cooking and they were all smiling. None of us had ever seen anything like it before, and our minds swam back four months to the less fragrant corridors of London's zoo.

Before we got to the cooking part we were invited to load up with individual packets of cereal, great jugs of cream (proper cream, the sort you cannot buy in America today in case you get a heart attack), toast, honey, piles of butter and toast and individual bottles of milk.

Lunchtime later confirmed that this was the standard set for every meal, with unlimited fruit and steaks and salads. As the only physical labour at the Polaris Flight Academy was walking out to an aeroplane or to the road to Los Angeles to thumb a ride, the good work of Babbacombe was soon eroded. Pay was two dollars twenty-five a day, which was about four times what we had been getting in England, and as we were not allowed to spend a cent off the camp because of the generous hospitality, even the dough was O.K.

At some 7,000 miles from headquarters, we were surely one of the more distant R.A.F. stations in the world. We were certainly the softest and most luxurious. But there, above the lawns and flowerbeds, fluttered the proud flag of the junior service, the R.A.F. roundel against a blue background—though above it, and quite right too, floated old glory, the stars and stripes.

This improbable Flight Academy was presided over by two amiable officers, a squadron leader and a flight lieutenant, who gently and smilingly administered the undemanding routine. What else could they do but smile with a permanent billet like this in the heat of war?

The ground instruction in subjects like navigation and engineering was looked after by Americans of liberal persuasion from the University of Southern California. Their task should have been totally agreeable, especially as they were paid well and did no more than a few hours a day, but one young man in particular suffered pains of conscience because he thought he was merely refining cannon fodder. (I suppose he was right in a way because only one or two of my batch who completed the course survived the war.)

Between the two hangars, where a couple of dozen biplanes were lined up, looking like Sopwith Pups behind the Western Front in 1917, life was grittier. Here a bunch of toughs, hell's angels every one of them, taught flying, and knew and cared nothing of cannon fodder. They were, almost to a man, ex-crop dusters or stunt flyers from Hollywood, survivors of many a mock battle high above the clouds, and many a simulated gory air crash. Most of them limped heavily and there were few unscarred faces to be seen. They had been issued with rather smart brown uniforms, with fancy brass wings on the chest, and sleek forage caps. Often unshaven, and with oil-stained old shoes, they looked like wounded tramps who had been partly redressed by some charity in Army surplus uniforms.

Our Flight Commander was a heavy, handsome and un-scarred fellow with a more sophisticated air about him. His name was Bud, or Buddy, and he claimed to be the beloved brother of the famous star of the silent screen and America's sweetheart, Mary Pickford. We were told he 'checked out' students for solo and grades.

I was given a sandy-haired little tough with a broken nose. He had been a crop-duster since 1927 so hardly knew what it was like to fly above twenty feet, and the worries of his life had created deep lines which in turn filled with the dust of his calling. His close-set eyes were angry and blue, and he cursed all the time, with much spitting. 'Goddam it, Hough, get the stick over for Chrissakes!' he would scream in the air. He talked to me down a rubber tube and the spit would work its way back into my ears in times of great passion.

'Goddam it, I'm going to throw you around the goddam sky!' were his first words to me. This was entered in our log books as 'Air Experience', and I suspect that it was designed to test our nerves and air sickness. After my North Sea and Atlantic experience I did not believe for a second that I would survive.

We strode out together across the dusty tarmac to one of the stringbags. They were all struts and bracing wires and doped canvas surfaces with the ribs showing through like a hungry dog. They were painted bright yellow. 'That colour stands out when they're looking for the goddam wreck,' explained my instructor reassuringly.

A tiny bit of perspex protected you from the worst of the wind's buffets. Inside the cockpit you were festooned with straps over thighs and under arms and across the chest for the parachute and the safety belt, both with complicated and mis-named quick release clips. And then on your head you had a padded helmet with goggle straps and those beastly rubber tubes for carrying spit and expostulations. They had to be plugged in, and when you turned your head sharply they could part sharply too.

Once you had got the hang of taking off and landing, flying was really very easy, much easier than driving a car. If only you could just leap joyfully into a cockpit, press a starter button and off you go. But there were overalls with map pockets in the thigh where the maps were tight-folded and inaccessible. And the parachute harness always got in the way. To get at the map you had to take off leather gauntlets, holding the stick between your knees while you did so, then your knitted gloves, and finally your silk inner gloves. Then they all fell to the bottom of the cockpit, far out of reach. You then jerked out your map, un-folded it if it hadn't now blown away, and folded it to show the bit of ground you were interested in. But that was five minutes ago and you had travelled some seven miles and the railway station you had picked out as a good landmark had long ago disappeared behind.

All this is very fussing and a grave disincentive to flying. No wonder a lyrical writer about flying has yet to emerge. Even Richard Hillary and Saint Exupéry don't quite count, and everyone else has been too busy fiddling and fussing with the paraphernalia, too distracted by minutiae to notice things like the slant of the sun across a hill's undulations at dusk, or the flash of intermittent moonlight on cloud tops and piercing its way through gaps to the sea below.

Recently I did some flying again, and though the flying side was nothing, all the wires and straps and preparation and checking and getting permission and complying with the multitudinous regulations put me off for the last time.

Here I digress, even before I am airborne for the first time. When I was I began to regret it because my crop-duster really tested that aged biplane, and me, to the limit, with a series of strut-cracking, stomach-turning evolutions, from rolls off the top and snap rolls to spins. I was far too terrified to be sick, and was not, goddam it, allowed to touch the controls. 'We'll do it again tomorrow,' threatened my crop-duster.

It was ludicrous that anything as primitive and prehistoric as a Stearman PT 13 (primary trainer) could assume demonial qualities. In fact it was as innocent as your first fairy-cycle, with no vices, great forgiveness and strength, and nice responsiveness to your wishes. Nice plane, nasty instructor. Flying instruction is not a profession celebrated for gentleness, good manners and patience, and I was not the only one of the course to become half-paralysed with fear of these scarred, cursing American instructors.

By contrast, their actual flying, their treatment of the controls, was hypersensitive. It was a curious experience to have the controls taken out of your hands with some violence and much cursing, and then to witness the delicacy with which this middle-aged tough would sideslip the Stearman down and by delicate stages bring it to earth without a jolt.

The Mojave Desert winds could become ferocious, getting up in a rush before the little Stearmans already in the air could be warned. Then the fun began as the mechanics deserted the hangars and everyone went out to line the runways and then run out to hold the planes down as they landed backwards, their stalling speed being far below the wind speed.

I don't remember any accidents with those Stearmans. You had to be an awful ass to crash them. One boy on our course did some illegal low flying and took away some high tension cables with his undercarriage, blacking out the town of Bakersfield. He was on the next train back to Canada. A dozen or so more of the fifty didn't show enough aptitude and were sent home, too.

'For Chrissake, Hough,' my crop-duster barked one morning, 'get out and solo the goddam ship.'

It took the strength of two mechanics to crank into life the 120 hp Continental engine. When it was running smoothly on both magnetos, I signalled away the chocks with heroic nonchalance. In front of me my instructor's cockpit appeared alarmingly empty. I had learned to detest the very shape of his head over the nine hours I had stared at it in the air—the way it swivelled from side to side as I came gliding wobblingly down towards the ground, and swivelling right round when the expletives were exhausted. The blue blaze of his eyes behind his goggles was like a ferocious dog fight clip from *Hell's Angels*, and he could actually pitch his voice above the sound of the engine and wind.

The Stearman could take off by itself. That was no problem. But there are few more final acts in life than opening wide the throttle of an aeroplane when you are sitting alone in it for the first time. It has to be done. There is no escape. The blue of the sky above you will claim you as the very blackness of nemesis on your deathbed. The hereafter is almost all speculation, with only two certain alternatives: you must either separate yourself from this ton of metal and canvas, or bring the beastly thing back to earth with you inside it.

After three circuits of the airfield, I decided bravely on the second course. I could see the khaki dots of my fellow cadets, white faces pointing skywards in eager expectation of catastrophe. Floating ridiculously in space close to me, two more lonely souls awaited the coming of the same courage and inspiration which must soon bring them down to earth again.

I cut back the throttle through its quadrant, and when the starboard wingtip coincided with the goddam landmark my instructor had earlier pointed out, banked and slipped at a hideously steep angle towards the strip of tarmac.

As everyone knows, the act of landing an aeroplane, be it the Wright brothers' 'Flyer' or Pan-American's 'Jumbo', consists of causing it to travel progressively more slowly until it can no longer support itself in the air and has therefore to be supported by the ground. The switchover of responsibility must, as far as possible, coincide with the wheels being close to the ground. If you lose momentum too early the aeroplane drops through

25

space, too late and it bounces up again eager for more flying. Both lead to bad landings. If they are very bad the aeroplane breaks.

My first solo landing was unique in the annals of aviation because it combined both misjudgements, according to terror-struck eye-witnesses, and led to *three* rapidly successive landings. My memory, even immediately afterwards, was dim because my eyes were tight shut. However, I lived and the wheels were not crushed, and later I was even able to taxi the good, brave old Stearman back to its parking place.

That evening I celebrated by buying an old radio in the nearby township of Lancaster, and lay on my bed listening to Artie Shaw and Duke Ellington and pondering on my ever more dangerous future. Then my thoughts turned to the golden city beyond those hills, forbidden territory to us flyers when airborne, but wide open and hospitable on the ground—so we had been told. Tomorrow leave began, and at 4.30 hellbent we would all be for the glitter and glamour of movieland.

In the fall of 1941 the glory of Hollywood was undimmed. Untouched by war, by television and the tyranny of the liberal conscience, the movies reigned supreme as the Queen of American Entertainment—and of world entertainment for that matter. Garbo was mysterious, Ginger Rogers healthy and dancing, Deanna Durbin healthy and singing and bicycling, George Sanders was the supreme cad, Basil Rathbone the supreme detective, Peter Lorre the supreme bogeyman, Humphrey Bogart the supreme tough. Aimée Semple Mac-Pherson hot-gospelled in her incredible temple, Ronald Colman gave elegant, discreet afternoon teas, and ennoblement was placing your dainty white foot into damp cement outside Grauman's Chinese Theater.

At first nights unbelievably glamorous and famous and sanctified super-stars descended from Cadillacs in white mink amid gasps and hushed cheers and the flashes of a hundred

26

cameras. Moguls who could break or make a star overnight scanned through sheafs of glamour-pix with hooded eyes, the ash from their fat Havanas falling like grey snow onto their bellies while they made up the cast for the new epic. Every drive-in restaurant, every drugstore, sported as many lovely girls as you could find in any London chorus—all drawn here by the lure of the silver screen and the hope of a glimpse of a casting couch.

No European court, not even the court of the Sun King himself, can have equalled in grandeur and romance and predatory self-interested manipulation, the courts of R.K.O. and M.G.M. and Paramount during those golden years. No Commines or Burleigh held more power and influence than those vitriolic and relentless gossip writers Hedda Hopper and Louella Parsons.

By happy chance in my first war campaign overseas I caught a last glimpse of all this while serving my King and country in southern California. I viewed some of the poshest movie star mansions—not for me the goggling through the windows of a tourist coach. I was there, right in the front line, movie star in one hand, highball in the other. I could be found at the Little Mocambo on a Saturday night, drifting in a Lincoln along the Sunset Strip in the wee small hours, sauntering hands in pockets past the guards into the very heart of movieland, the sacred studios where, it was said, even Cecil B. de Mille had to show a pass.

I became familiar with the touch of mink against my arm, the scent of Chanel as I danced on moonlit balconies, the flash of lightbulbs as more pix for the fan-mags were snapped of me in the company of the great.

That was the life for me—when I was not fumbling about with a Stearman's joystick at 6,000 feet, being bawled out by an instructor who had somehow failed to recognise the new-found status of his pupil.

It is no credit to me that I became adopted so early by the

stars of the silver screen. It all began, willy-nilly, in a golf club. The English in particular among the film colony were feeling a shade guilty about living the good life in the land of steaks and sunshine while their less fortunate countrymen back home were experiencing rough times. The least they could do, they decided, was to put on a good show for the troops. Or rather, Ronald Colman decided. For Ronald Colman (and only a very tight inner circle called him Ronald and *no one* Ronnie) was the squire of British Hollywood, and had been almost since his arrival seventeen years before.

Ronald Colman had landed in America with twenty-five dollars and the self-cast part as an English Gentleman. He had played this part off the sets without a break, and on the sets with hardly a break, ever since. His smash-hit start had been opposite Lillian Gish in *The White Sisters*. From this epic, through the Bulldog Drummond series and *The Prisoner of Zenda* he had not turned his elegant head to look back. He lived with his second wife Benita Hume in what appeared to be the largest country club in Surrey, magically transplanted to Beverly Hills, complete with ivy and virginia creeper outside and fumed oak panelling and cretonne covered armchairs and curtains inside. The gardens were marginally smaller and less elaborate than those at Kew.

Ronald Colman carried out his squirearchal duties as if he lived in The Grange, Tilford. He applied delicate pressure to ensure that the right people, and none of the wrong people, came to the Church Bazaar and the local Anglican church, joined the cricket team and attended the charity bridge parties. It was discreetly made clear that it was the ultimate honour to be invited to dinner at the Colman home and no one ever refused. Tennis parties were attended only by those with unsullied (or nearly, for Hollywood, unsullied) lives. Only the older and very best and very famous American actors and actresses (the word film star had never crossed his lips) came to his home, and brash upstarts like, say, Victor Mature or

Veronica Lake, would never see his azaleas in bloom nor taste his cucumber sandwiches at 4.15 p.m.

Like any good English squire, war had greatly added to Mr Colman's responsibilities. Bundles for Britain afternoons saw to it that tins of good Texan meat and once-worn frocks were on their way to the old country, and Benita Hume and other wives had stood loyally by Lord Beaverbrook's appeals for old aluminium saucepans—and no one had asked how much it would cost to ship *them* 7,000 miles to Britain by way of U-boat threatened convoys.

Hints were dropped to some of the younger, fitter Englishmen that Britain had her back to the wall, old boy, and perhaps it was time to answer the call to the colours. 'We don't want to lose you but think you ought to go' sort of stuff. They did go, within a week most of them, and almost to a man. The worst exception was Errol Flynn. But then what could you expect of an Irishman who *drank* and did not even want to be a gentleman.

When we lads in blue began to turn up it was clearly a squire's duty to see that we received proper hospitality. There had also been some heavy hints from the British Embassy in Washington to spur on the locals' natural hospitality. With this in mind Ronald Colman Esquire (it said so on the invitation) and friends requested our company at a party at the Beverly Hills Golf Club. . . .

The British colony had clubbed together to entertain us for an evening, and no host or hostess was to be absent: Mr Colman indicated so. Not that pressure was really necessary in this case as doing your bit for the boys was just becoming fashionable, and soon (after Pearl Harbour) it would become *de rigueur* and the stars would be fanning out all over the world to sing and dance or just look pretty for the boys and make them laugh and whistle.

We arrived at the golf club in a coach, all rather spotty and adolescent, on a mellow moonlit night, tumbling out half awed, half defiantly determined not to be awed, into the floodlit entrance.

Our hosts and hostesses had wisely arrived some time before us in order to get adequately tanked up. As we drifted blinking into the main lounge, there they all were, not an unfamiliar face to be seen, the only party I have ever been to at which I have known *everyone*.

And all our hosts and hostesses, I realised, were rather larger than life. For there was Basil Rathbone, more sleuthlike than Sherlock Holmes, and in neat juxtaposition, Nigel Bruce, more of an asinine duffer than Watson could ever have been— and with a bigger pipe. So genial, so hearty, yet somehow wrong in black tie: where were those thick, heather-scented tweed plus fours?

And who was this—and this? No, it couldn't be true. Myrna Loy and Ida Lupino in long sequin dresses and sparkling like a Rand diamond mine, turning to greet us with their breathtaking smiles. Artur Rubinstein was there to knock off a few tunes, and Alan Jones (already swaying like a storm-buffeted poplar) to sing for us, and no doubt it would be 'The Donkey Serenade'.

Reggie Gardiner may not have been a name on everyone's lips but I recognised the jolly fellow at once, and all had certainly heard at one time his famous train noises.

Hard liquor flowed like Niagara, to the detriment of my fellow airmen, but on the whole to the improvement of the film stars, some of whom were surprisingly shy at first. I saw one or two of the guests being helped out of the lounge even before the buffet supper, and I found myself making anxious excuses for them.

Charles Boyer was in his best amorous mood, floating mournfully about the room as if half broken by love, head slightly tilted, muttering endearments to all in his seductive French accent. 'Ah, mon ami,' he whispered to me, 'you are all so 'andsome airmen all the girls in London must be in lurv with you.'

I stuttered rather stiffly that I was in fact engaged and didn't

30

dilly-dally with any old girl around. To prove it I took Charlotte's photograph from my pocket and showed it to him. 'Ah, ma foi, I onderstand—what a beautiful girl!' His words were a caress and I felt like crying. 'Will you permit me to send her my special lurv?' And he took out a gold pen and wrote signed endearments on the back.

Charlotte was pleased to have this later, but I think she must have been a bit put out by some parts of my account of this affair. 'Olivia de Havilland was the most lovely thing there,' I wrote. 'Venus-like figure, sweet innocent face, charming to talk to. I got more intimate with Maureen O'Sullivan,' I continued unabashed, 'who is also perfectly glorious with very refined voice—a sort of female Charles Boyer. I wanted to get a picture of me talking to her to you and thought by concentrating hard we might do it. . . .'

I do recall now sitting on the floor with this heavenly creature, half behind a curtain, having a go at thought transference, her latest hobby. It required some long periods of silence and the tight holding of hands, which suited me fine. But, rather to my relief, nothing more intimate was proposed of course.

No thick velvet curtain could insulate us from the sound of the merry party beyond. The stars were holding up remarkably well considering. Myrna Loy giggled divinely when I asked if I could count the freckles on her right hand, and then let me. It was that sort of stage of that sort of party.

The dancing was beginning to flag, mainly because there were so few airmen capable of standing; so we had some impromptu entertainment by those best equipped to offer it. 'Come on, Allan,' I heard Brian Aherne call out. 'Let's have it.'

'Hear, hear,' cried Brian's petite, fetching new young wife Joan Fontaine.

'I say, Allan old boy, I think you ought to give it to the troops.' It was the voice of Ambassador Colman. But to Allan Jones it might have been the voice of Haig at the Somme giving the order to go over the top—an order that was not relished but was to be obeyed.

Ian Hunter and a laughing Edna Best helped Allan up onto a table, but not carefully enough because he fell before he was upright. Amid much merry laughter he was thrust up again, and with Rubinstein banging out the tune on a not very good piano, Allan Jones went superbly into his 'Donkey Serenade'— 'There's a song in the air, but the gay señorita . . .'

'He puts on a jolly good show when he's had a jar or two,' commented C. Aubrey Smith.

In the brief interval before the next impromptu act I asked Brian if he knew John Collier the script writer and short story writer I was trying to contact on the grounds of mutual friends in London. He said he did and would drop me a line. 'And Joan and I would simply love you to come for a week-end some time. . . .'

'That's very kind of you,' I stammered. He surely couldn't be serious!

There were one or two recitations after this, and Rubinstein worked his ivories through 'The Moonlight Sonata' which had several of the ladies in tears. And then, just as the evening seemed to be at an end—as well it might at 4.30 a.m.—Reggie Gardiner decided to steam out of Euston Station, and then across the points into Primrose Hill tunnel. 'Clickety-clickety, clickety-click . . .' and the whistle, the changing note into the tunnel.

All our hosts and hostesses must have heard it a hundred times, but they demanded an encore. Reggie needed no encouragement, and he was beating his way up the long incline to the round house—'chuff, chuff', and the shriek of skidding wheels—for the fourth time as we began to drift out into the moonlight.

My contemporary account becomes quite lyrical here: 'And outside the moon was shining on palm trees waving gently in the breeze and long sleek shining cars and white fur capes and long slim figures, and the air was scented and below were the

32

ten million lights of Los Angeles and far away the great snow-capped peaks.'

I was especially aware of one lovely dark figure gliding approximately towards me on a zig-zag course. I intercepted her. It was gorgeous Kay Francis, with whom I had earlier danced several times. She had seemed rather melancholy and I had tried to cheer her up. Now I said to her (rather pointedly, come to think of it), 'Do you by any chance know of a cheap hotel near here where I could spend the night?'

It was rather like asking Barbara Hutton if she knew of a good cut price drug store. But if Kay was in the least put out, it was quite concealed by her sweet kind nature, or perhaps by her alcoholic condition.

'My dear boy, you must come home with me.' And she took my arm and I navigated her towards the biggest Cadillac I could see. My guess was right. Her Negro chauffeur gave her some tactful assistance on one side, and with me on the other, in she went and I followed hard behind before the door could be slammed.

In the dark, seductive rear of that limousine I was over-whelmed by the mixed scent of Night and Day and good malt whisky. 'Of course you must come and stay with me,' my new friend and hostess repeated.

'Gosh!' I exclaimed, and groped for adequate words. 'This is terribly kind of you. You could easily drop me at the Y.M.C.A. if this is too much trouble.'

In fact it would have been a great deal more trouble as we were rapidly and silently ascending the canyons of Beverly Hills into Bel Air, that most exclusive of mogul residential paradises where only the mountainously rich lived at that time, and Los Angeles's Y.M.C.A. was at least a dozen miles in the opposite direction. So, with her lovely dark locks spread over the silk cushions, she said in her deep voice, 'What a lovely party! Wasn't darling Allan just too superb? The tighter the better with Allan.'

'Gosh, what a party!' I agreed.

We slid past some white gates and the tyre note changed from tarmac to deep gravel, a sound I have always thought profoundly reassuring. It went on being gravel for quite a long time before a vast white mansion hove into view, looking very fairytale in the moonlight. When we eventually reached the porch my heart was throbbing up and down like the Cadillac's eight pistons. What was expected of me now? Brian had confided in me that she was not currently married. Was I going to be seduced or was I supposed to be doing the seducing? For a panic-stricken second I regretted my cheek and thought of those uncomplicated bunks down at the Y.M.C.A.

Then a young lissom man sprang from the shadows of the porch as we drew to a halt. One of the many manservants? With mixed relief and disappointment I heard his voice, and it was not speaking as a manservant spoke, even in this egalitarian republic. 'Kay darling, you *have* been a long time.'

He was a saturnine lad, in his late twenties I guessed, and in my incredible innocence I imagined that he must be a young nephew. He accepted me without any questioning or much interest.

'God, I need a drink,' was Kay's jocular response. And she meant it. I meekly followed the pair through some unbelievably vast rooms, all hangings and drapes and six-seater sofas, to a bar bigger than the Crillon's. The nephew set up three giant highballs with un-nephew-like efficiency, and Kay and I recounted in turn the goings-on at the golf club. 'Oh, all those pilots, they were so sweet and so brave,' said Kay in a dreamy voice. 'I kept thinking of them fighting for their country, high in the sky, against the German hordes. I love your country,' she said, turning her tenderest smile on me and then draining the last drop of a second highball.

At last Kay Francis became practical. 'We're going to put you up in the attic, I do hope you'll forgive. I've just rented this place for a while until my new house is finished, and the bedrooms are all filled to the ceiling with my furniture.'

34

We spun round on our bar stools and made for the stairs, through four more rooms, each decorated in a different period. The staircase was like one of those which Ginger Rogers and Fred Astaire used to trip down before their dance routine. Kay needed the full generous width as we made our way upwards, although she remained as articulate as ever with ne'er a slurred word. Up again we went to the attic floor, identifiable by marginally lower ceilings, and the young man—whose name I never learned—flung open proprietorially a polished mahogany door and followed Kay and me inside.

That last highball had all but done in my brain, but what had survived counselled caution. Had we become, suddenly, a *ménage à trois*? A glance in the direction of the giant mock Elizabethan four-poster suggested that there was accommodation here for several *ménages à trois* or even *quatre*, which was confirmed by the size of the golden bath I could see through the open door of the next room. There were funnier goings-on in Hollywood, weren't there? So I had been told.

The young man disappeared and to my relief Kay was suddenly brisk and hostessy again. 'There's whisky there if you need a nightcap,' she pointed out with a steady hand. 'And cigarettes—and that's if you get hungry in the night . . .' indicating a silver bowl of fruit. 'Come and have breakfast with me in the morning.' A last whiff of 'Night and Day', a chaste brushed kiss across my cheek, and she was gone with a whisper of silk against silk.

At 10 o'clock the next morning a gentle knock on my door was followed by the appearance of a bent, grey-haired Negro manservant who told me that Miss Francis was ready. Ready for what? After sloshing some water over my face in the gold basin, I followed him down to her suite on the first floor to find out.

A heavily alcoholic sleep had finally dispersed all belief in the reality of last night's fairy tale. Yet here was Queen Titania again, and lovelier than ever, I saw, when I had covered the

35

quarter mile to her reclining throne. Her face that millions idolised looked up at me from the silken pillows and her lovely white arms were spread wide in welcome. Before her on a bed-width tray lay her breakfast—a small measure of tomato juice in a dainty cut-glass.

'How did you sleep in the attic, Dick dear?' she asked in her deep rather husky voice and as if in regret that I had been alone.

The manservant brought in a man's breakfast, flapping open a sheet-sized Irish linen table napkin across my shaking knees.

'I have to be busy today, isn't that a bore? Can you amuse yourself with one of the cars for a while? I've fixed you a perfectly glorious girl for the opening night at Earl Carrol's tonight. And then we can have fun tomorrow when I'm not so boringly busy.'

I thought that sounded O.K. as a programme overture, and later sauntered into the garage and picked myself a baby Mercury a mere 16 feet long and ventured forth onto the boulevards of Beverly Hills.

The girl in the evening *was* perfectly glorious, as promised— I have her photograph to this day and I suppose she is now a granny many times over and wouldn't dare to wear a bathing costume. She didn't then, either, but for a different reason. She was a chorus girl and in those unenlightened times a chorus girl touched with the merest shade of brown, let alone a white strap mark against brown, was instantly dismissed—which was a bit hard in sunny California. I remember her as being a rather simple soul, and I also remember only too keenly that she had a chaperone in the large shape of the manageress of Earl Carrol's, the world's greatest night club.

The three of us sat at a ringside table, the girl demure and silent, the manageress studying the shape and movements of her chorus girls with dispassionate judgement, like a critical works manager considering the production flow on a new and little-tried machine. Her comments were as sexless and clinical as his might have been—like 'Sheila's getting more knock-kneed with every show—she'll have to go', this of some angelic specimen with four-foot-long legs.

We went backstage and met them all over a celebratory bottle of California 'champagne'. I carried away an impression of numerous identical, white, gum-chewing robots who spoke reluctantly and then only in twangy monosyllables. Even at the susceptible age of 19 I was quite unmoved by this mass of pulchritude. Is it the same today behind the scenes at bunny clubs?

Kay had promised 'fun tomorrow', and so it was. It began with another jolly breakfast with my gorgeous brunette hostess, who at last began to understand that I was not after all a much-decorated hero of the Battle of Britain and only a just-soloed cadet. To her even more marvellous credit, this in no way diminished the enthusiasm of her hospitality and interest in my well-being. Then a prolonged frolic in the swimming pool, followed by lunch at Romanoffs.

Romanoffs at lunchtime was *the* current Mecca for the very very famous in Hollywood. It was kept exclusive by the simple method of refusing table reservations to anyone who had not got a star billing in a major movie and charging prices that only the very very rich could afford. (A slice of melon cost a dollar sixty and cocktails began at a dollar fifty—regular New York prices today but astronomical thirty-five years ago.) Romanoffs was also kept very dark and very private by thick curtains which shut out all the California sun and replaced it with candlelight.

Our luncheon began badly. We were early and there were only a few people to waggle a discreet gloved finger at. At the bar there was a half-slumped figure.

That carrot-eating night fighter ace 'Cat's Eyes' Cunningham could not have matched the probing capacity of stars like Kay, who could pick out a fellow celebrity, friend or enemy, in pitch darkness and cigarette fog at fifty feet.

She recognised her old friend Salvador Dali and greeted him

37

with a merry quip. There was no response and I saw that his long thin fingers held a pencil and he was slowly doodling triangles on a menu the size of a suburban front lawn.

She put an arm round his bowed shoulders and repeated her greeting, and very slowly he swivelled his head round. The tips of his famous moustache were twitching like a cow's tail on a hot summer afternoon and his dark pop eyes stared dully—no 'Cat's Eyes' was he—and without a trace of recognition straight at Kay. He gave me a brief hostile glance and slumped back to his task.

Quite un-put out, Kay withdrew her arm, put it through mine instead, and as we walked towards a large round table in an alcove, remarked cheerfully, 'Poor Salvador! Such a dear, too, even though he refuses to speak a word of English.' And she went on to tell me about the scenery he was painting for an M.G.M. film.

Romanoffs soon began to fill up and my eyes began to pop and swivel like Dali's. The experience was rather like studying stills of some all-star epic outside a cinema in the blackout. Everyone knew everyone. 'Darling Kay, how are you?' I heard a dozen times and dutifully jumped up and down for the introductions. 'Do you know Merle Oberon?' Kay would enquire as if there might be some doubt about my answer. 'Do you know Joan Bennett, Dick?'

And each in turn—I blush to mention it even today—responded thus, or something very like it: 'My, a real live R.A.F. pilot! How many Germans have *you* shot down?' And it was no good trying to explain because of course young Englishmen are just too too modest for words.

One by one this parade of the élite sorted itself out, some draping themselves over the bar, others settling round the tables. About eight joined Kay and me, among them Herbert Marshall and his very pregnant wife, Reggie 'chuff chuff' Gardiner and Merle Oberon.

'Where's Ginger today?' someone enquired, as if she was the

only very very famous film star absent—as indeed appeared to be the case. 'She's gone to her ranch,' a voice from the next table replied. It belonged to Errol Flynn, tanned, tough and terrific, and soon—though he did not yet know it—to acquire notoriety by 'liberating' Burma from the Japs single-handed.

Otherwise attention was centred upon me, of all people, and they kindly enquired about Winston Churchill ('He's quite well, thank you'), how often I had been bombed out, and did I have a regular date back home and similar riveting topics. I could not understand why they should be in the least interested in me and my trivial life.

The dry martinis and tom collins's flowed fairly freely all through the meal—no wine—and the atmosphere became nicely relaxed and Reggie Gardiner began to get up steam again for that long climb out of Euston station, which coincided with the coffee.

'Now what?' asked Kay of the table at large.

'Shopping,' said Merle decisively.

'What would you like?' asked kind Herbert Marshall, and I answered laughingly, 'Well, first some gramophone records. Then a cigarette case because American packets get so squashed under your parachute harness, and . . .'

Reggie Gardiner whistled, crossed some points and rose from the table. 'So be it,' and he took my arm and led me out into the blinding sun, the others following soon after. By the time they had caught up I had been propelled into a nearby shop, a Beverly Hills version of Aspreys, and to my horror had been *bought* a cigarette case—not actually solid 18 ct gold but a very nice and obviously very expensive one.

'Right, next stop Crewe,' he responded to my protests, and, with a whistle and hiss of steam, we made our way across the boulevard. This time Herbert Marshall was in the lead, limping fast (he lost a leg in the Kaiser war). 'Anything you like, old boy,' he said, sweeping an arm expansively towards the ceiling-high racks.

Merle Oberon laughed at my open jaw and said, 'Grab 'em while you can, airman.'

Prodded on irresistibly, I took a 12-inch Bunny Berigan, a Fats Waller, an Artie Shaw, and I think one more. That was my Stalingrad, and I held firm. 'Well, you're a modest lad,' remarked Herbert Marshall, and nodded towards a bowing salesman. Credit cards had yet to be invented but a famous face was better, and I never saw a film star pay cash or cheque for anything in a shop.

A famous face also attracted attention for there was nothing blasé about the citizens of Hollywood and Beverly Hills, and there were many faces flattened against the window glass before we left. At the door autograph books were waving like banners in the afternoon sun and I signed a few with a flourish that was soon to become practised and instinctive, before slipping into Kay's limousine beside her.

The others waved good-bye and darling Reggie pushed one more record through the open window. 'Just for you, old boy. Couldn't bear you not to have it. Toodle-oo!' And he clickety-clicked away.

I looked at the label. 'Train Sounds by Reginald Gardiner' it said.

'You ought to have got him to sign it,' said Kay. 'But I expect we'll meet him again soon.'

'You mean our lines may cross at Crewe,' I quipped. That's what Romanoffs did for you.

3

Bud Pickford had a swashbuckling, Rabelaisian style and a racy reputation in the Antelope Valley, and it was said that every farmer's wife had known the warmth of his bear-like embrace. To some he was even known as 'the flying seducer'. Bud was a practised dropper-in, timing his exploits with the advantage of height. Antelope Valley farms were large and well-scattered and visibility was always unrestricted.

Sometimes Bud would go off alone. 'I'm gonna test that ship,' he would be heard to announce to the chief mechanic, who knew as well as Bud that that ship had been passed O.K. as to airframe and engine only hours before. 'I didn't like the sound of that motor you were running up this morning.'

He assumed a special seducing step, too, as he strode out across the tarmac to the innocent Stearman. There was a new lightening of his bulk and a new vigour to his swing onto the lower wing and into the rear cockpit. He would make a pretence of testing the magnetos, shaking his head in doubt, then taxi straight out. Fifteen minutes later, if you knew his ways, you might find him hovering at six thou. like a kestrel, goggles thrust back searching for the tell-tale cloud of dust from a labouring tractor which, if it were distant enough from the homestead, gave him the all clear. Then, no dive bomber has spotted his target with keener eye nor descended with more unerring aim.

Later he began to combine duty with pleasure. I was one of

the first to witness his expertise at first hand, so to speak, when I was having my check-out for the next flying stage of the course.

'Goddam it, Hough, Mr Pickford's gonna check you out this a.m.,' my instructor barked one January day, 'and he don't want no shit from you, goddam it.'

'No, *sir.*' And off I went with my lumpy parachute, three flying suits, gloves, gauntlets and helmet and goggles and maps and the rest to Bud's office.

I did not let on to Bud that we must have many mutual friends over in Beverly Hills. Even at a raw nineteen I realised that was injudicious. If I had done so, I should have missed one of the more interesting occasions in my Hollywood war.

I was too awestruck and too concerned with giving the right answers to his searching questions about navigation and airmanship as we walked out to our ship to recognise his seducing step. But others did and told me later.

'O.K. Hough—take her away,' I heard him order down the speaking tube, and I made a moderate take off with no more than a few bumps back to earth.

At two thousand feet I heard his voice again: 'O.K., I'll take over.' Bud took us to six thou., doing a climbing square search at the same time, paying the same attention to the ground below in search of a friend as a good fighter pilot pays to the sky above in search of his enemy.

At a farm close to the edge of the Antelope Valley Bud found his target. Until that moment I had only half-believed the tales of his philanderings, which had sounded too good to be true. On that fine morning I was to learn better. It was as if he was on some lone mission, that I was not there at all, a mere phantom pupil pilot.

There was a tractor working among the orange groves a good three miles from the farmhouse, and down sped the dreaded libertine of the Polaris Flight Academy. With engine just ticking over, he sideslipped with astonishing skill the last thousand feet and put down without a jolt and in twenty-five yards, concluding his run within the same distance from the back door. He was out while the wheels were still rolling, kicked a rock against one of them as a chock, and yelled to me, 'Stick there—I gotta visit to make.'

So there I sat, clutching the vibrating edge of my cockpit, hoping the chock would hold, and slipping instantly into my Captain Ball world. 'Huh-huh-huh . . .' hand hard on the trigger. 'Huh-huh-huh—there's the Red Baron in his red Fokker triplane. Get in a quick three-second burst with the Vickers, and down goes the tripehound, a lick of flame sprouting from the engine. . . .'

Bud returned with remarkable speed, a glow of satisfaction on his well-filled face, and still zipping up the front of his flying jacket. He ducked under the whirring prop, a kick sent the rock clear of the wheel, and while he was slipping his bulk into the front cockpit he yelled, 'O.K., let her go.'

I might have asked 'Let her go where?' But I knew he could only mean that I was to take this contraption of wood and canvas off into the air from the bumpy, scrubby bit of ground ahead of us. Captain Ball would not have hesitated. No more would Hough.

I pushed the throttle wide open, flicked the top of some bushes with the wheels, steered round the farmer's water tank, and licked off some of the sweat that had trickled from under my helmet. Bud, I now noticed, was quite relaxed. He had not even bothered to strap himself in and was returning to his hip pocket a modest flask of Bourbon.

'You did well, boy, you did very well,' he told me back in his office. 'You'll go on to Basics next week.' I thought I had seen some pretty good basics today.

'Goddam it, Hough!' exclaimed my instructor. 'So I'm finished with you, goddam it.'

I should like to have met the woman Bud claimed as his sister, who had of course been married to Douglas Fairbanks and lived in an estate of prodigious dimensions they had called Pickfair. She still does. But over the following weeks my social life beyond the hills flourished happily. I spent another week-end with Kay, and then accepted with alacrity an invitation to stay with Brian Aherne and Joan Fontaine while I was at Kay's house. 'Darling Brian,' commented Kay. 'You'll have fun there.'

Kay's chauffeur dropped me off at 703 North Rodeo Drive early one evening. I sized up the dwelling with practised eye. Modest, quite modest compared with what I had become accustomed to. A nice bit of open lawn at the front, double garage, pillared portico, green-shuttered windows.

The Filipino butler Frank opened the door and stared at me in some bewilderment. I learned why later. R.A.F. uniform was still almost unknown in Beverly Hills and I had been told to my face that I was a Guatemalan Marine by one authoritative night club drunk. For poor Frank the situation was complicated by the fact that his mistress was at that time playing the part of a W.A.A.F. in a film called *This Above All*, and left for the R.K.O. studios every morning in a W.A.A.F.'s uniform. If I was a male version of Joan Fontaine I must be playing in the same movie, but I was definitely not Tyrone Power, even Frank could see that.

I further confused things for the poor fellow by saying, 'Kay Francis told me I was invited for the night with Joan Fontaine.' But it got me past him and his inscrutable Charlie Chan eyes widened perceptibly.

I had a good look round while awaiting the return home of my hostess. It was a more manageable place than Kay's, I mean you didn't actually wear yourself out walking around. The swimming pool occupied most of the back garden and there was a generous balcony running the width of the house at the rear.

Nice plants, a cared-for feel, domestic and homey. I approved. The bar was nice, too. There was a welcome bit of pub influence

44

about this movie star bar. Dark oak panelling, leather-topped bar stools, hand-embroidered cushions on a sofa, copies of *Punch* lying about, pewter mugs lined up on a shelf ready for the noggin.

Only one wall was very un-pub like. It was covered with signed portraits of matinée idols and notable women of the theatre and celluloid, each photograph lit to flatter facial cragginess, and signed Basil, Errol, Doug and Nigel. The women—Norma, Greta, Miriam, Marlene and co.—were equally narcissistic. And, funnily enough, there was a huge bowl of dozens and dozens of narcissi on a table under them—neat juxtaposition—see plate 4b.

I heard the merry sound of my hostess's arrival and nipped back to the drawing-room, pretending to read *Life*. Joan came in with a light bounce, a chit of a girl of twenty-four, in slacks, sandals, loose blouse, and with her face plastered in make-up. 'Hullo, old chap,' she greeted me. 'So glad you've come. Let me mix you a drink.'

She did so with great dexterity, a Pimms with many fruity ingredients, and slid it across the bar to me. She put her hands up to her white-plastered face. 'Whoops! I must get this horrible stuff off. Make yourself at home. Relax. Have another drink. Play the piano or write dirty things on the walls.'

I attempted a manly laugh and buried my nose in the mug as she tripped away. Half an hour later I heard her dialling the telephone in the drawing-room. 'I'm just calling up Brian,' she shouted at me. 'He's in San Francisco. Help yourself to drinks.' Then, 'Operator, I want . . .'

Brian Aherne, I later learned, was forty. He had married Joan only recently. For both it was for the first time and they were madly in love. I had seen on the grand piano a photograph of them, he tall and manly, striding out of the church, she petite and floating beside him, whitely diaphanous.

'How are you, darling?' asked Joan in that appealing, vulnerable voice the whole world had succumbed to in *Rebecca*.

'I miss you terribly.' There followed a lot of gossip, especially about Darryl Zanuck. Darling Darryl, to whom she owed so much.

After a quarter of an hour and a distant protest at her extravagance, Joan said a little sulkily, 'But, darling who's making all the money?' The answer was, alas, she was—1,500 dollars a week, which was not bad for a comparative newcomer to the business. And Brian was not actually making a film at that time. If I had been more worldly I might have spotted future trouble here.

Joan Fontaine had style. She also had pace and self-confidence and a brittle masculine manner which brooked no nonsense and concealed a generous heart. If she had been brought up under more orthodox circumstances she would have led her guide troop with panache and made a killing of the rosettes at the pony club gymkhana.

In fact she had been born in Tokyo, like her elder sister Olivia she had followed to Hollywood before the outbreak of war in Europe. She had worked in the rather menial task of chauffeuse, make-up girl and general aide-de-camp to famous film star Olivia until David Selznick had recognised her appeal and offered her the lead part opposite Laurence Olivier in *Rebecca*.

The call had come on the fifth day of her honeymoon, to the despair of Brian. And the petite, fun-loving wife—described later by Brian in his memoirs as 'young, pretty, gay and utterly charming'—became a major film star overnight. Neither her elder sister nor her husband was too pleased about this.

In Brian's absence Olivia turned up to spend the night at 703 North Rodeo Drive as a sort of chaperone as it was thought unseemly for young, blonde, beautiful film stars to be sleeping alone in Beverly Hills mansions with young airmen. Hedda Hopper, who was even bitchier than Louella Parsons, had got her hat-pins into the de Havilland girls at that time and it was deemed politic to reduce to the minimum any opportunities to

46

attack them. In fact she did all the same and in a vitriolic paragraph linked poor Joan's name with a British airman—'pleasures for the troops', something like that.

Olivia was chubbier, slower and less electric than Joan, and she had accepted an American accent which Joan kept at bay for almost all her Hollywood career. I knew nothing about their relationship but did notice that they appeared to be rather guarded with one another and not noticeably sisterly. But they were both vivacious and polite and kind to me, asking the usual stuff about poor old war-torn Britain, what flying was like, where I lived, did I have a girl and all that jazz. There was a good deal of booze and I remember being kissed goodnight as if I was a nephew to whom they ought to be kind, although in fact Olivia was only six years older and Joan four years older than me.

Olivia's bedroom and mine were separated by a bathroom which we shared, with a good deal of pre-arranged knockings and lockings. I had never shared a bathroom with a film star before, nor heard one at her ablutions. They were impressive and prolonged, and when I got the double knock it was after midnight. Inside the air was heavy with scent and bath salt emanations and steam. There was powder on the floor and jolly panties lying around. It all seemed a long way from the Wilmslow latrines, vomit-stained blankets and troopship odours.

Brian arrived from San Francisco later the next day and Joan threw herself into his arms. He was tanned, fit and hearty and offered me the same warm welcome that Joan had given me—nice, casual, matter-of-fact hospitality. The tempo of the morning built up steadily. An American colonel who seemed to know Olivia very well indeed arrived in a large car, and in ones and twos members of the British set, and some Americans too, turned up. Also a notable Frenchman and his wife. M. et Mme (Pat Paterson on the screen) Charles Boyer were very *entente cordiale*.

Jon Hall looked a gay dog, with long black hair for his lead in *Aloma of the South Seas*. John Loder was fit, lean and talking golf hard. The Surrey cocktail party element was best represented by the Herbert Marshalls. Poor Mrs Marshall was more pregnant than ever and could really only manage to sit in the shade alone reading *Punch at War* on a sort of swinging bed. She was relieved of her burden the next morning.

Heather Angel and another semi-starlet were as pretty as could be, and darling Heather's capacity for Pimms was spectacular considering what a slip of a thing she looked. Whether or not George Sanders had actually been invited was a subject of some speculation. Certainly the coterie of little starlets he had in train, and who settled down around him like chattering sparrows, were not on the visiting list.

'Always late at the studios,' Mrs Nigel Bruce divulged to me in shocked tones. 'Such a trouble, poor George. Not a *proper* actor really. He reads his part, you know, from blackboards,' she whispered over her pewter mug, and paused to check the lie of the land. 'He is quite improvident, too, you know, Dick dear. Spends all his money just now on toy trains—would you believe it?'

The sun blasted down and some of us dived into the pool and scrambled out for more Pimms. There was war talk but it came in dutiful parentheses, and for the rest it was gossip among the women and sporting talk—cricket and golf mostly —and anecdotage among the men. The afternoon drew on and people began to look at their watches to ready themselves for the evening cocktail parties and the dinner dates that followed them.

'Thanks awfully again for that message to my fiancée,' I said to Charles Boyer who I now regarded as an old friend.

'A pleasure,' he purred. 'Sans doute we shall 'ave the pleasure too of seeing you chez Colmans tomorrow for the luncheon?'

I looked blankly at him until Brian came to my rescue. 'Yes, old man, we'll all be at the Colmans.'

'Cheerio, old boy,' chipped in Nigel Bruce, and he tucked in his pipe again and rolled away like a Dutch cog in a swell, skimming an unprotected corner of the pool before starting the long climb up the two steps to the balcony.

It was not to be taken lightly, this business of getting ready to go to the Colmans. Clothes, car, timing, all had to be thought out carefully.

In the end Joan wore a sort of baggy Chinese style (Chiang Kai-Shek was a goody then) trouser suit, her fair hair in two short pigtails, and Brian standard British slacks and tweed sports coat. We left Frank behind and Joan chose to drive the Packard rather than the Mercury. A nice compromise.

On the way the homes of some of the notables were pointed out to me, and as we did our zig-zagging up the canyons towards the mountains and the mountainously rich, I caught an awesome glimpse of the white stone facing of one wing of a stately palace. Brian turned in the front seat and pointed it out. 'That's Ginger's place. She'll be coming.'

'Just for the drinks,' added Joan, 'though she doesn't drink actually. There'll be quite a few for the drinks.'

Never mind about the numbers, I told myself, my heart hammering away like a Stearman's radial. But Ginger Rogers! Now that really was a bonus bonus. Ginger—the love of my boyhood! The great, marvellous, the talented, exciting and fabulous Ginger!

I remained in a state of stunned silence until the ivy and virginia creeper and good matured British brick of the Colman home came into view and we swished into a discreetly concealed car park among the rhododendrons. Those airy Bel Air sounds of distant splashing and whacking of gut against ball told their own happy tale of wealth and comfort.

We sauntered across the lawns and presently a superb figure came into view. I had seen him only amid the smoke and confusion of the battle of Beverly Hills Golf Club. He had been a calm commander then, but now it was nice to see him (so to speak) off duty. His tread was measured and the welcoming smile revealed the most famous set of teeth in the world.

His tread was also given tone with shoes by Lob, ordered by the dozen, flannel bags with geometrically precise creases, single breasted tweed sports jacket, and indefinably patterned silk scarf in place of what I had no doubt would have been a Guards' tie.

Ronald Colman's grey hair was brushed back just so. And that pencil-thin moustache! Now I could believe what I had been told so many years before, that one twitch could send a million female hearts racing. Elegant, authoritative and masterful, here was a gentleman straight from Dornford Yates. Or almost.

He bent down slightly towards Joan and touched his lips against her cheek, then turned to me. 'How very nice of you to come,' he said. His grip had the right strength—the strength of a man whose swordplay was only equalled by Douglas Fairbanks', and yet he was conserving his strength like any good ambassador who has *so* many to greet. 'Now you must come and meet some of my friends.'

They were standing around in casual groups about the lawns near the house taking drinks from proferred trays. It was not quite my first time, of course, but the blaséness of later months had by no means set in. Especially knowing that my Ginger was somewhere.

And the sense of unreality crept over me again, so that I had to pinch myself awake and remember that I was an airman at war. These affairs were more like a stroll through the pages of a fanmag than parties. On every side there were stars of the silver screen, smiling, pouting, playing their parts of innocence, childish cheekiness, worldliness, careless charm or fallen woman. A real live moving movie.

I tried not to study Carol Landis's legs too hard—or at least not as hard as I used to study them in *Film Parade* by torchlight under the bedclothes. Then Maureen O'Sullivan's soft

Irish eyes turned their radiance upon me. 'How *are* you?' she asked, forgetting our thought transference session. 'It must be wonderful to be alive after all that you have been through.'

I, too, thought it was O.K. to be alive, but did not add that the thrill of shooting down Messerschmitts must be as nothing compared with being looked at and talked to by glorious you. Instead I muttered, 'Oh, it was nothing really,' and became speechless, unlike Cary Grant strolling by who filled in quickly, wisecracking away in his cockney accent, which seemed very wholesome and homely in this fairy-tale land. Cary spotted Joan and gave her a jaunty wave—many a co-starring embrace they had shared recently in Hitchcock's *Suspicion*.

Distantly beneath a magnificent magnolia I spied my golden Mecca, my target for today, my Ginger. The waiter had brought her a giant milk-based concoction and as she took it from the tray she turned and laughed at something with Joan Bennett and I thought I would die on the spot.

Yet now was my chance, by gum. I edged nearer, but before I could get her within my sights I was intercepted by a positive squadron of British hearties who closed in and blocked my progress, waving their pots of beer, asking how things were with me, old top.

C. Aubrey Smith was the most ebullient, but he was closely matched by Ian Hunter, Nigel Bruce and Basil Rathbone again, with Herbert Marshall closing in limpingly from the rear.

'I'm one short tomorrow—care to fill in?' C. Aubrey Smith asked. And there was a shocked silence when I asked what for, or at? 'Why, his cricket team, of course,' Ian Hunter explained quietly, knowing how sensitive C.A.S. was about it.

I said I would be delighted to, and how awfully sporting of them it was to ask me.

'Good show, old chap.' There were flecks of froth on his splendid moustache. 'The other half?' he asked, reaching for my drink, pausing momentarily dismayed at my martini glass. Young chaps didn't drink martinis.

As he moved aside to look for a waiter he revealed to my questing gaze the magnolia tree. No Ginger. Then, far away with Ronald Colman at her side and holding her arm, I saw the back of her lissom figure in loose blouse and slacks moving with swift dancer's steps towards the open door of her Cadillac. Foiled.

We, the élite, the special guests who remained when the others had gone, had a long, light, luscious lunch on the patio. Ungracious and ungrateful as it may seem, I registered only two impressions of it.

The first was a sudden anxious outburst from Ronald when he overheard his wife boast laughingly that she had stowed away in the cellar several sacks of sugar against a rainy day and possible rationing.

'Benita, this is terrible!' Ronald exclaimed, with a theatrical frown upon his face and measuring his words carefully. 'What would happen to my reputation if this were known? This sort of thing gets around, you know, and though I flatter myself that I am without enemies, there are many malicious tongues in Hollywood.'

Benita apologised abjectly, and Ronald added less fiercely, 'Just get rid of it—that's all. And quickly, please.' His lips opened into the Monte Cristo smile and the teeth dazzled and the world was warm again.

The second impression was Ronald's monogram, which was impressed everywhere. Nothing seemed to be immune, not even the cigarettes, each one bearing proudly the diamond-shaped monogram with the letters R C, blue on gold. The place settings, the Pimms' glasses, the table napkins, matchboxes—wherever you turned there was no escape—R C R C R C.

I popped down the last of the crêpes suzettes and nodded to the waiter as he leant over my shoulder with the bottle of Très Belle Grande Champagne Cognac—both of which I thought passed muster and helped to dispel the gloom caused by the loss of Ginger. But the dark clouds were quite rolled away as quickly as they had rolled up when by chance I over-heard a happy remark. We were sauntering around the estate after luncheon, down to the pool, a glance in at the greenhouses and the upper tennis courts, when I heard Joan's voice from a few yards behind.

'Did you know Ginger's having a party this evening?' she asked Charles Boyer, 'and we're all to come. She's calling it a tea fight, of course.'

'How charming!' was M. Boyer's murmured response.

'Wizzo!' I whistled to myself.

After that agonizing meeting with Ginger across her milk bar, that ultimate climax of a climacteric Hollywood war, and the humiliating defeat that ensued, I played golf and cricket badly and left Beverly Hills with the awful feeling that my glam life with the stars of the silver screen was over for good.

But, who knows, I thought as I hitched my way back to the Polaris Flight Academy the following night—who knows, I might yet meet again my wonderful Ginger? After all, I *was* an airman, too. Perhaps I had not bailed out over the white cliffs of Dover. But I could loop the loop and slow roll with the best of 'em.

And DID GINGER KNOW THIS? I kept asking myself. There was only one way to prove it. Still heavy with highball fumes, I stumbled out to my ship shimmering on the hot tarmac, climbed in and scrambled off with the gusto of Captain Ball after a Pfalz. Without hesitation I headed south for the hills and the white temple of my goddess. I had drawn an unsteady line across the map and placed a firm cross on the area of the canyons of Bel Air where Ginger lived.

It was bumpy over the dry, hot hills, and the flight was taking much longer than I had expected. But at last, with my fuel gauge registering almost half empty, the land below became more domestic and I spied several splendidly grand estates far below.

Flying a bit sloshed and hung-over is very like flying at 25,000 feet without oxygen. Both conditions fill you with an abandoned sense of wellbeing and optimism. I was therefore confident that I should have no difficulty in locating for certain Ginger's white mansion amid the trees and succulent lawns and blue pools of Bel Air. I even convinced myself that the little figure sitting alone on the grass—perhaps musing on that young pilot she had met all too briefly two nights before—might guess I was the pilot of the little yellow machine buzzing high above her.

Now was my chance to show Ginger that I, too, was a real airman. So down I dived, the wind screaming through my struts, pulling back on the stick until my already sore head seemed to be pressed into the top of my spine. Half blacked-out, I put the stick in an approximate imitation of an Immelmann.

Instead, I was left stalling. A wing dropped, and I was in an involuntary spin at far too low a level for comfort. Kick opposite rudder—I just remembered that in my panic. And push forward the stick, hard. It seemed an unnatural thing to do, but sure enough, magically and undeservedly, I was drawn back from the jaws of death, and found myself skimming low over the Spanish tiles of the palace of my beloved.

Only God and Aimée Semple MacPherson, who must have been praying for me, knew how I escaped. But, by golly, I told myself as I quiveringly regained height, Ginger must have been impressed by *that* show of daring aerobatics. Who knows, next week-end when I was back in movieland I would meet her again?

'Did you,' I would ask casually, 'happen to see a plane looping over your house last Tuesday? It was me, you know.' A modest chuckle, a shrug of the shoulder. 'I just happened to be near your place and thought I'd show you a spot of spinning.'

Alas, the next week-end brought me only bleak news. I did not meet Ginger again, for on the Monday she had left for her desert ranch and the rest she so richly deserved. I had been risking my neck over a palace without a princess. Brian told

54

me of her absence but I did not tell him why I had enquired. He was a bit of a pilot himself and had warned me several times about the temptations of showing off and low flying.

America's entry into the war at first touched us only slightly. I had been standing on the top of the cliffs at Santa Monica— about the nearest point to Pearl Harbour—when the news of the attack came through on the radio. We cadets were rather superior about the whole business—'Well, you had it coming to you,' 'Now you'll know what it's all about.' That sort of thing.

We observed rather patronisingly their half-hearted and wholly unsuccessful efforts to black out Los Angeles. It was called a dim-out and it wasn't even that. And we observed rather despisingly the panic that followed the first reports from Hawaii, with drivers piling up their cars on Sunset Boulevard as they succumbed to heart attacks.

But the eating, drinking and playing habits of Californians remained unchanged. Packards and Cadillacs swished along the freeways, which were already presaging the age of private urban mobility which hit Europe fifteen years later. And the colourful cycle of hard fun and hard work, booze and gossip kept the films churning out from Columbia, 20th Century Fox, R.K.O. *et al.*

Joan remained hard at work. She got me onto the set of *This Above All* where I watched her being a W.A.A.F. and made them change the buttons on her tunic which were all wrong. She was doing a sequence with Tyrone Power and Tommy Mitchell, and she went on doing it again and again, all in that rising ground mist (blown onto the set with little fans) which characterised Hollywood films about England.

After she got her Oscar as best actress for her part in *Suspicion*, she went on triumphantly and apparently unspoiled to a 20th Century Fox production of *The Constant Nymph* opposite *mon ami* Charles Boyer. I watched that being shot too and

55

began to feel more and more like a film extra and less and less like an R.A.F. airman.

For some reason I never understood the flying course became more relaxed after Pearl Harbour and we got longer and longer leaves, and were told that we might not get back to England until mid-summer 1942. But, at about the speed of a Wright biplane, we worked our way through Basics, which were very boring Vultee planes with neither performance nor character, and onto Advanced.

The AT6—or 'Harvard'—was a gorgeous little machine, offering for the first time real style and speed. 'Wait until you get on Advanced,' we had been told as we grumbled our way through Basics. And this was right. Now we had retractable undercarriages, and the Wright-Cyclone engine allowed us to cruise at around 180 mph and take her in a dive to around 250 mph.

A big new flying school was built in the nearby Mojave Desert with the pace and urgency America threw into her own defence work after Pearl Harbour, and we would meet their silver AT6s on long cross-country trips far down to the Mexican border and the Colorado river $3\frac{1}{2}$ hours away. But there was the same sad absence of brotherly spirit between us in our blue uniforms and the American Army Air Corps in their khaki uniforms that we were to see more seriously on active service later in the war.

I remember only one co-operative episode, and that was a melancholy enough one. A whole course of 25 Americans had got caught in a freak snowstorm close to the mountains, and five machines had failed to return. Several of us, now senior pilots at Polaris, were deputed to help search for the missing ships. It was for me the first occasion of purposeful action and I remember taking it very seriously, doing square searches over the foothills of the Sierra Nevada.

Suddenly I caught a glimpse of a tiny grey splash just below the snowline on a steep slope, and I reduced height to a few

1a Stearman Primary Trainer PT13 (*left*); North American Harvard Advance Trainers AT6 (*background*); and Vultee Basic Trainers BT13 in the hot California sun, 1941.

1b Night flying outside Hollywood.

2a Rare cloud over the Sierra Nevadas on the way to flying below sea level at Salton Sea with Allan Palmer.

2b First hesitant efforts at formation/photographing flying. Both camera and film were Joan Fontaine's presents.

3a/b Two bluff Britishers of the Hollywood film colony in 1941. Nigel Bruce (*left*) and Herbert Marshall.

3c The discreet shaded home of Ronald Colman, millionaire squire of British Hollywood in 1941.

4a Dashing, romantic Ronald Colman with luncheon guests, Joan Fontaine on his left, Mrs Charles Boyer and Brian Aherne with back to my camera. Benita Hume, later Mrs George Sanders, is on the extreme left.

4b Pimms Number One and decent beer were the most popular drinks at the Brian Aherne/Joan Fontaine bar.

5 (*opposite*) Kind hostess Joan Fontaine dries her Nicky in the sun. She had just won her Oscar for her lead in *Suspicion* with Cary Grant.

6a Sunday swimming before the guests arrive at North Rodeo Drive. Brian
Aherne, the host, is about to take the plunge. Beside him his sister-in-law
Olivia de Havilland, with very good friend.

6b Cadet Hough, in borrowed tennis gear, about to take to the
court. The winter of 1941–2
was a relaxed one.

6c Pretty little Heather Angel with pretty
big Pimms.

7a/b Hangover dawn at Ludham after an eventful 21st birthday party.

7c Typhoon 1B at Coltishall. H for Harry saw me safely through the busy autumn of 1943 but was herself a bit knocked about.

8a Rocket Tiffy. I preferred bombs.

8b A brief honeymoon break in the Lake District in July 1943.

hundred feet over it. It was my first sight of death and catastrophe, and I circled it several times in a thoughtful way, watching for any sign of life from the flattened spread of glinting aluminium and oil stain. All the planes had had instructors on board as well as pupils, but it was impossible to see any evidence of life or death. Later we learned that none of the ten had survived.

By diving down on the wreck several times I succeeded in drawing the attention of some cowboys nearby, and when I had to leave for lack of fuel they were heading towards the scene of the disaster.

We reached the conclusion, perhaps an unfair one, that the Americans panicked more easily than we did in an emergency. I don't think there is any evidence for this when they are training, and certainly not when they are qualified and experienced. But I do know that at that time, when flying aids were crude, they did not relish flying at night. Our course included some twenty hours of night flying, and when the time came for this period our instructors became tense and snappy and grabbed any excuse to scrap flying for the night.

It was a curious experience to see these tough, scarred veterans flinching from the darkness. But their fear, real as it must have been, was not transmitted to us. On the contrary, with this chance to show our mettle we became defiantly injudicious. We were no longer raw amateurs ourselves and we tried to bully our instructors to go off into the darkness with us against their better, if rather timorous judgement.

But no—if there was a cloud in the sky, flying was cancelled for the night, and we returned crossly to our bungalows.

With two hundred or so hours in my log book I was becoming over-confident. This is a dangerous period in flying training when valour easily wins over discretion. I had made friends with a dark, good looking boy called Allan Palmer. I not only introduced him to the pleasures of Beverly Hills but egged him on to unlawful flying about the desert in our lovely silver

Harvards. We taught ourselves formation flying so that when we came to it officially on our course even our hard-boiled instructors had to grunt reluctant surprise at our speed in picking it up.

I saw on the map that to the south of the Mojave Desert there was a salt lake that was shown to have a minus altitude. Allan and I set our barometric pressures correctly and flew together down there one hot afternoon to see how far below sea level we could fly. Salton Sea, as it is misnamed, showed up as a white expanse of salt long before we reached it—so blinding that it was difficult to get any perspective as we reduced height.

Needles on dials have always fascinated me. I remember the ecstasy of watching the Smith's speedometer needle on our 1928 14/40 Humber move towards, then touch and edge just beyond, the 60 figure as we tore with a following wind across Shropshire. And the Kaiser War altimeter I carried around in a rucksack moving over 3,000 feet climbing up Helvellyn. It was now with singular pleasure that I watched my Harvard's altimeter needle register a minus figure.

But I gave the dial only the briefest of glimpses as it was very difficult to judge how close we were to the salt surface flashing glisteningly past our wingtips.

Allan came down to join me and we had a short game of dare, pushing lower and lower. We were showing minus 280 feet when we reached the limit of our daring. From the altimeter I glanced at Allan fifty feet away, the shadow of his plane almost the same size as the Harvard, we were that close. We laughed and then pulled up in unison, our throttles wide open.

On another day we decided to visit Mexico, which was only 180 miles distant, and we landed on a short and bumpy airstrip just over the frontier. I snapped a rather saucy photograph of a mounted frontier patrol, which took not the slightest interest in us, before taxi-ing across the scrub and taking off.

There was a certain degree of secret kudos attached to these unauthorised long flights, especially as they had to be over very basic desert if you were not to be spotted, and in case of any difficulty you were liable to be dehydrated in no time. (The desert wind was so dry that you could wash out a shirt, hold it up and put it on again all within five minutes.)

The course's long distance record was held by the inevitable clown who flew a reverse compass bearing on a navigational exercise that was supposed to take him to Pasadena. Instead, with nothing in sight but rocky outcrops and burning desert, he finally ran out of fuel in the middle of Death Valley. He was, luckily, picked up by a rare motorist, but by then was feeling and looking like a loofah.

It was the only mishap on our Advance course. The planes were very safe and well maintained, and visibility was almost always unlimited, so you had to be a fool to get into trouble. About 36 of our original 50 were still left, and there were no more failures. On the whole the weaker pilots were among the older men—those grizzled middle-aged fellows of 23 and 24.

The ground work ground on boringly. Our eggheads from U.C.L.A. were much too soft and permissive to keep our attention and when it came to the final wings exams it was obvious that half of us were quite unqualified to sit for them. There were in fact just 50% failures, inevitably including me. The remedy was simple. In order to hold on to their soft jobs and avoid the draft, our instructors sat amongst us when new papers came from headquarters three weeks later and ensured that this time there was a 100% record.

But that was still all before us when we were given another ten days leave in March, and Allan and I hitch-hiked around California, up to Yosemite Park to ski and swim and bask in the mountain sun. Then back to the good life in Beverly Hills.

Again there were big parties and little intimate parties, tennis tournaments at the Colmans' house, ten-pin bowling, or just swimming and night-clubbing. The hospitality was limitless. I have the minute-by-minute record, in an old letter to Charlotte, of one evening with Joan and Brian:

Started off with dinner at the Bit of Hungary and ate queer things. Then up to Ginger Rogers's house to see if she'd come with us but she was in bed with a head so went to Mocambos where we joined up with Louis Hayward, Ida Lupino's husband, and Ilona Massey and an American general. Mocambo's is on Sunset Boulevard which runs along the edge of the foothills and there's a marvellous huge curved one-piece window which gives a panorama of all the Los Angeles lights.

Dancing with Joan to an all-negro band among the palms in the very dimmed light with the glittering lights below was something you only get once or twice [I continued to Charlotte of all people. And then added as a sop] But don't worry, I was pretending it was you and some day we'll go there and do the same thing. About ten pictures were taken of us and some will be in the Movie Mags.

Went on to Slapsie Maxie's which is a lower joint and was very crowded so we didn't stay long; then to the Little Troc which was raided the week before because they ran a gambling place up in the mountains and kept a fleet of cars to take customers to it. Like all night clubs it was very dimly lit and terribly cramped—all-negro band and a truly wonderful negress who hushed the whole place (that takes some doing) by singing Embraceable You and several blues numbers in a delicious husky voice that shook everyone up because of the feeling she got into it.

After the third of her songs Brian asked who she was and no one seemed to know. 'You've got young eyes,' he said to me. 'Can you read that?' He passed me the outsize menu which I tilted towards the candle. And there at the top in letters smaller than 'Smoked California Salmon' was 'Guest Artiste Lena Horne'.

60

'Never heard of her. But she's got something,' Joan conceded.

Another new discovery in Hollywood at that time was singing with the Benny Goodman band. Dancing one evening at the Palladium with some gorgeous blonde I came to a grinding halt when the voice began fluting its way through the first ballad of the evening. Later I wrote home to Charlotte, with the same absence of tact, 'Benny Goodman has got a new singer. She is called Peggy Lee and I'm madly in love with her.'

Frank Sinatra was swinging his way into his fab career as a crooner (they were still called that), a cadaverous, hungry lad who had my partner screaming her head off with the rest instead of teaching me how to jitterbug as promised.

Among the dazzling stars listening to one of Lena Horne's first evenings at the Little Troc was a plump, homely figure, already struggling with a weight problem. It was my first glimpse of enchanting Deanna Durbin. She was at the height of her remarkable career in acting and singing, most notably singing on a bicycle. We exchanged inaudible hullos with her on the way out and that was all.

My last week-end in Beverly Hills coincided with my twentieth birthday, and Joan and Brian gave me a lovely party with a specially baked cake, complete with loving message and twenty candles, at an immensely grand place. Then on to dance at a Chinese place characterised by spasmodic and startling simulated tropical storms, complete with the sound of rain on a hot tin roof and the whistle of wind through palm trees.

There was a third call at a very diminutive place with a dance floor that continued out onto a balcony with hanging lanterns dimly lighting it. I remember my last dance with Joan here, and then, miraculously it seemed, there appeared my very favourite mother-figure of the golden screen, that Simone Signoret of the 1930s, Claire Trevor.

Claire was more up to expectation than any other expectation I had experienced in Hollywood, and what a suitable night for it. My 20th birthday! Manhood at last! The moon was shining, the cicadas were clicking (they may, I suppose, have been simulated too), Duke Ellington was playing, I was full of lovely food and drink, and I had Claire Trevor in my arms.

All the time we whispered endearments into each other's ears. 'Oh, how I love you!' whispered she; 'Oh, me too, how I love you!' Then at the end we broke apart smiling and she held both my hands and burst into deep laughter. 'I am also very happily married, have children I adore, and shall love for ever my darling husband.' (I believe she did too, lucky man.)

Then, still both laughing, we walked hand in hand back to the table where Joan asked briskly, 'What's the big joke?' Then to Brian and me: 'Come on, chaps, time for sleepies. I'm a working girl.' And off we went in the purring Packard, down the Sunset Strip at sunrise . . .

Earlier in the day, after tennis with Ronald Colman, he had shaken my hand for the last time. 'Good luck, young lad,' he said, and I knew from his voice that he meant it. 'Mind you shoot down a lot of those Germans, eh?'

'I'll do my best, sir,' I replied stoutly, resisting the powerful urge to salute.

There was a last flash of teeth. 'Good show!'

And so it had been.

4

I took a drab photograph of the Canadian frontier from the train. It shows a wire fence six feet high and, beyond, a bit of uninteresting grass and some anonymous trees. The train did not cross it for many miles and I dozed off. When I awoke we were over the border and the fairy tale was over, too. Soon we were back in Moncton transit barracks, now stained with the passage of thousands of airmen instead of being raw from premature birth.

Already the war was becoming a reality again. Royal Canadian Air Force police were in evidence, we were no longer the select few ripe for local hospitality, and everywhere there swarmed new sprogs fresh from Britain, more callow, of even lower physical and mental calibre, even spottier, than my contemporaries. We rejoined the other half of our course, whose reward for passing their Wings exams first time at Polaris was to rot in this unpromising encampment for more than three weeks while we failures lived it up in the California sun.

The *Duchess of York* took us home from Halifax in eight days in early June 1942. It was a smooth, warm passage, uneventful except for a number of abortive U-boat attacks. This time, with three stripes on our sleeves and glistening wings on our breast, we had cabin accommodation, shared with veterans of the Desert war, dark-tanned and whistling 'Lili Marlene'.

Bomb-battered Liverpool docks made a fitting entrance to England again after the tranquillity and luxury of Beverly Hills. Our training, which was to be so thorough in some respects and so perfunctory in others, took no account of the dizzy-making switch from one extreme to the other. One minute, it seemed, we were one of a small and élite group; the next an anonymous unit in the vast R.A.F. clearing house that was Bournemouth, almost as low in the scale of service vermin as we had been a year earlier.

Like the flats in St John's Wood, the luxury blocks in Bournemouth had all been taken over by the R.A.F. and converted into barracks. (Where, for goodness' sake, did all the inhabitants go? It is one of the Hitler War mysteries.)

There was leave, and Charlotte was more delicious and more fun even than I had dreamed during all those months of separation. She was working at the A. P. Watt literary agency but wanted to join one of the services. 'No, no, no,' I appealed. 'Not that!' The little cottage in Bushey in Hertfordshire where she lived with her mother, who had more or less adopted me since my parental semi-defection, was a haven of welcome, warmth and understanding. I must have tested their goodwill sorely with my lyrical tales of the glamours of Hollywood in my letters, comparing England so unfavourably with California. But now I made some small amends by emptying a kitbag full of silk stockings and tins of butter and fruit and meat onto the tiny cottage lawn.

Those long week-ends and long leaves between stages were gone for ever. The R.A.F. spent the war with either a desperate shortage or an embarrassing surplus of aircrew. In the early summer of 1942 there was something of a panic on. I had only a brief leave before being hustled away onto my next Advanced Flying Unit course, and when it began we worked for ten to eleven hours a day, seven days a week, with a twenty-four hour break once a fortnight. Flying took place in all but the foulest weather.

64

Watton was (and is) a large permanent R.A.F. station in Norfolk, north-east of Norwich. Over the following years I moved airfields many times. Sometimes you arrived by air, but more often by train, and the last mile or two in a lorry or on foot. I know of nothing more distinctive and memorable than a wartime airfield. To the outside world they may have all looked the same. To anyone who was going to live there for a while—and maybe die there—each stamped its nature indelibly on your mind.

Most had an ominous demeanour, especially those like Watton with great dark camouflaged hangers with their zig-zag roofs and steel girder extensions like gibbets at each corner to accommodate the giant sliding doors when they were opened. By the very nature of their function and unlike Army barracks, airfields were stark and open to the sky. There were few tall trees near them, and from a distance the first thing you usually saw was the water tower. Then the crouching hangars, the grey concrete control tower, then the living quarters and scattered Nissen huts, and last of all the olive drab aircraft themselves, widely dispersed about the perimeter in their bays.

It was the absence of bright colour as much as the destructive function of wartime airfields that contributed to their ominous character. If only Trenchard had ordered bright scarlet uniform when the R.A.F. was formed, with sparkling epaulettes and silver bearskins, then how much less characterless would the Junior Service have become. A touch of style and vulgarity would have done away for ever with the chips that have sprouted from drab blue R.A.F. shoulders since its 1 April 1918 formation all those years ago when men flew without parachutes and stringbags were stringbags.

Watton provided me with my first taste of a R.A.F. airfield. It was a hard, functional, ruthlessly busy place, like a town on the make, swarming with W.A.A.F.s and airmen. There were about a dozen of us on the course and Watton swallowed us and pressed us into its production machine. The Commanding

Officer glanced us over within minutes of our arrival, checking our shoulder badges and noting a Rhodesian and two New Zealanders. 'Quite a change to find no bloody Yankees,' he noted, to my dismay, for I was now fanatically pro-American and in any case it seemed a slighting remark to make of volunteers who thought, rightly, that they would get to the fighting quicker through the R.A.F. than the American Army Air Corps.

Before we could wash off our travel stains we were bundled into a lorry bound for the dispersals for flying. The machines were dual control Miles Master Mk. 11s, as unfriendly and ferocious aircraft as Harvards had been forgiving and stylish. These trainers had been all right as first conceived, but to bring the performance up more closely to that of contemporary single seat fighters an 870 horsepower Bristol Mercury radial engine had been installed.

Like a Mini with a Maxi engine, the fine balance was lost and the machine tended to take over from man. Someone who had flown both recorded that the Master 11 was as lethal as a Kaiser War Sopwith Camel, but I think he was exaggerating. At least—or at first—there was another pair of hands to help you out of any trouble.

Just as in California there had been two breeds of instructor, crop-dusters and stuntsmen, so here in England there were two breeds. The first was of pilots who had worn themselves out on operations and were fit for nothing else; the second, those who had decided that they would be serving their country better by training others, or, to be fair, were forced to do so. I started off with one of the former, a Canadian called Mara, a Flight Sergeant.

I can't imagine why I attracted such bad language in the air, except the obvious assumption that I deserved it. Mara's language made my broken-nosed Californian's seem very tame and limited in expression. His range of vituperation was truly wonderful, but at least he couldn't spit at me. Now we were connected by only a couple of wires, the intercom, and these wires could easily be unplugged if you needed peace.

After one long morning of simulated emergency landings on a satellite airstrip, at which I became worse and worse as the language became fouler and fouler, I suddenly screamed back at him to shut up or I would kick his stinking arse as soon as we landed. It was scarcely up to his standard, but its effect was instantaneous. I made a perfect three-pointer with a dead engine, just over the hedge, and his language from then on was as mellifluous and pure as a monk's—or almost.

A cursing instructor and a handful of a plane combined to make a difficult start to English flying. The third unpleasant surprise which again served to remind me that I had been dreadfully spoilt up to now, was the flying conditions. In California these had been ideal, with perfect visibility and mostly without a cloud in the sky. The wide open desert and the Antelope Valley had offered us immediately recognisable landmarks, such as small towns and large mountains, and just the right number of them. Dead straight roads and railway lines stretched from horizon to horizon. If, even then, you were stupid enough to get lost you switched on a radio channel which brought you the sound of a beam guiding you to the nearest major airfield.

Now it was a very unpleasant shock to discover that days when visibility was more than five miles were rare, that cloud base was often less than a thousand feet, and that the patchwork of romantic fields and meandering roads and innumerable villages in England called at first for total concentration in order to avoid getting lost—never mind about flying. Here you were expected to take off when the end of the runway was invisible and when, willy nilly, you were almost at once enveloped in cloud.

In peacetime, we were told, it was easy. You simply dropped down low enough to read signposts or the names on railway station platforms. Now all these had been removed in order to confuse invading Huns.

We got used to it in time, learned to follow the iron beam (or railway lines) and match its eccentric twistings with those on the map. But that first flight with Mara was a bewildering experience and caused me to wonder if I would ever be able to cope with this devilish machine and this maniacal instructor in this mist-laden atmosphere above a dizzy kaleidoscope of little fields and woods and villages. I would have to learn to fly all over again.

'Christ, that was godawful,' commented my Flight Sergeant encouragingly when we landed.

There was, as always, some help in numbers, however. None of my lot had performed very sparklingly the first time. It was a quaint aspect of R.A.F. philosophy, upon which I was often to ponder, that a pilot whether he was training or on a squadron, must never by the smallest hint be given any sort of praise or encouragement. On the contrary he must at all times carry the burden of knowledge that he was a ham-fisted, stupid and dangerous fool in the air.

I quite saw that praise, if it was ever earned, must be granted sparingly during training for fear of instilling over-confidence. There was never any danger of this. I wondered sometimes how many wretched half-trained pilots had killed themselves, overcome by panic in cloud and spinning in, or miscalculating fatally in landing or taking off from lack of self-confidence. This unsparing denigration of pupil pilots' ability certainly accounted for some of the truly ferocious number of casualties at the advanced training stage.

Boastfulness is an unlovely characteristic. False modesty isn't very nice either. I think the R.A.F. with its own youthful lack of self-confidence tended to overdevelop the second for fear of the first. 'Shooting a line' was the service's unpardonable sin and much R.A.F. practice was directed towards its suppression. It began with special enthusiasm during training and tended to over-correct and lead to an unreal world of euphemisms in which no self-respecting pilot crashed and was killed but had a wizard prang and went for a burton. It was at first all very puzzling and discomfiting.

I didn't much care either for the Americans' fairly frank assessment of their own abilities, which was so much at variance with the R.A.F. style and led to a lot of conflict between the two air arms. But the R.A.F. would have benefited from being a bit more straightforward and less loaded with slang to cover their fear of appearing to swank.

The speed and efficiency of the training at Watton were terrific. It rained heavily on most days but flying was rarely cancelled because of the weather, and we took off for formation flying, aerobatics and mock dogfighting—with ciné cameras instead of guns—in weather that would have had our tough Californian instructors cowering under their ready room tables.

The manner of flying was very matter-of-fact and no one argued about flying conditions or dared to reveal any sort of concern. 'Today was fun,' I wrote to Charlotte, 'an hour's flying in formation in the pouring rain at about 100 feet, just missing steeples and skimming roofs and taking away the tops of trees at 200 mph. . . .'

Low flying, to 'get under' the enemy's radar, and for close ground attack, was looming more and more importantly in action, and almost every day we were out, dual or solo, getting used to dodging trees and high tension cables and generally speeding up our reactions. From time to time someone overdid it and we were short of a face and an aircraft. We took it in turn to act as pall-bearers and attend the funeral. Early in July I was deputed to do this for the first of many times. It was a burnt case, and these were popular with pall bearers as the coffin was so light on the shoulder—so light sometimes that we felt obliged to put in some rocks.

The Luftwaffe was still coming over in small numbers, intruding at night to shoot down bombers landing after raids, and tip-and-run bombing with Messerschmitt Bf109s by day. 'Pull yer crate into a f-ing tight turn if one gets on yer tail,' my

Canadian instructed me. 'He can only stay a few minutes and he'll never catch yer like that.'

I had dreams of ramming the Hun instead, then bailing out, neat as can be, and sauntering into the mess that evening—my best relaxed Captain Ball gait—perhaps with some mud on my boots and a small graze on my forehead. 'Anyone would have done the same thing,' I would remark as the first beer was lined up for me by my goggling fellow pupils. No line shooting, of course.

Then one day there appeared at the dispersal a face from the past—a fresh, pink, softish face from the Polaris Flight Academy who had been eight weeks ahead of me in his training—just long enough to complete his instructors' training after his return to England. He was a Pilot Officer now, his shining uniform still carrying Moss Bros's creases. Pilot Officer Lundin was to take over from tough Mara for the last couple of weeks of this course. He pretended not to remember me from California and was very patronising in a soft-voiced sort of way.

Later in the morning while I was playing poker on the grass and waiting to go up, I caught sight of him bouncing down the steps of the Chief Instructor's office, swinging a 'chute in one hand, his helmet and goggles in the other. 'Right, Hough, it's low flying for you today. In you hop.'

The next ten minutes are as clear in my mind as the last moments of a convicted murderer before the rope tightens. I am not suggesting that I experienced any presentiment of disaster but the mind's power of total recall before the moment of disaster is remarkable. I have known it several times and it is always the same.

Lundin was impatient to be away. A bustler. He was already strapped in while I was fumbling my way into the front cockpit, and when I plugged in his voice was already saying, 'All right? All right?'

I said 'No!' firmly and fussed with my straps, trying unsuccessfully to tighten them. In front of me was the three-sided screen with the unprotected metal bracket to which a gunsight could be secured. Tucked away below it, the usual array of instruments—A.S.I. (air speed indicator), altimeter, oil pressure and temperature, the bank and turn indicator, and so on. And, horizontally below, the gyro compass.

The engine was already running. Lundin signalled chocks away and he taxied decisively and fast across the grass, calling out to me before take-off, 'I'll take it.' Full of confidence, he was.

It was not to be low flying for me. Nothing of the kind. It was to be low flying for him, to prove the inspired progress he had made since we had flown the same California skies. He banked low straight from take off and before the undercarriage had even clunked home.

Regulations demanded that low flying was practised only in the special low flying area, except for authorised cross-country flights. My green Pilot Officer, obviously a crop-duster *manqué*, disregarded all this and never went above a hundred feet until we reached Thetford forest. Then he put the nose lower and corkscrewed along, dipping first port then starboard wing to within a few feet of the treetops.

In my idiotic innocence I was not in the least scared. I was as impressed as he had hoped I would be. He might have decided to be only an instructor, but by golly, he was some pilot!

I was a touch alarmed when I felt a bit of tree quite distinctly strike our belly, and then really alarmed when, instead of lifting up he did the same thing again, more heavily. This time the engine at once conked out and the silence was sudden and pretty awful.

Only now did my brave instructor pull back on the stick in order to gain a bit of height and search for a nice place to put down. But Thetford forest is large and there wasn't even a clearing in sight.

'Looks as if we've had our engine,' remarked Pilot Officer

Lundin informatively. Then, 'Turn off the fuel, for God's sake.'

We ran out of momentum with astonishing speed and we were doing only about 130 mph when we touched more decisively the topmost branches of some oak trees. I remember thinking it seemed rather a pity and a waste—such a brief flying career and not even a sight of the Hun, let alone Captain Ball's score of 44.

Then the world became very noisy again after the silence, and successively first all green and then all black. . . .

It was the most divinely beautiful face I had ever seen, far exceeding in utter loveliness every film star with whom I had so recently been dancing in the glam night clubs of Beverly Hills. A cool hand was on my forehead—actually to staunch the flow of blood but I had no idea of that. I wasn't even particularly uncomfortable. I was lying on the edge of a ditch and the smell about me was a compound of oil and bracken—not unpleasant, reminding me of mechanical trouble with the old 14/40 Humber on a picnic in Ashdown Forest.

The face was smiling down at me in some anxiety. 'Is there anything you'd like?' asked this heavenly creature.

I tried to say 'Cigarette', but there was something wrong with my lips. But this girl had incredible intelligence as well as incredible beauty. She knew what I wanted at once and felt in my pockets.

I did not follow much of what was going on and I saw nothing beyond her face. For that moment in the no man's land between life and death she was my whole world. I felt the cigarette between my lips and I drew on it clumsily but with some satisfaction. Then to my deep disappointment her face faded from view, never to be seen again, and a black curtain was drawn again across my eyes.

I never even knew her name and though I searched for her when I was better I never found any trace of her. The plane had torn through a number of trees and finished upside down, and, by a remarkable stroke of luck, with the cockpit resting laterally across a drainage ditch.

Perhaps she had been working in a field and had seen us come down. More romantically, I later imagined her on a lonely picnic, reading Browning or Wordsworth, when she was so rudely interrupted. Whether she was a landgirl or just a poetess taking a walk, she was remarkably brave and tough. The risk of fire had been very great. But on her own she somehow got us both out of the wreckage and pulled us on to the bank. Perhaps she then went for help. I shall never know.

Lundin was lying on the other side of the ambulance, his eyes closed, groaning slightly, a large swelling and bruise on his forehead. He had concussion but no other injury. Once he opened his eyes and smiled. 'Wizard prang!' he remarked. Then later, and ominously, I thought: 'Don't forget, the engine packed up. . . .' That was all. I couldn't speak and closed my eyes.

The next time I opened them I was installed in bed in considerable mental and physical pain. The facts of my situation were as follows, though I was not to learn of them until later: from the feet up, I had cut my shins, ruptured some ligaments in the left knee and cracked both knee caps, ruptured some muscles across the small of my back (much the most painful of the injuries), lost some teeth, cut my face, broken and knocked skewwiff my nose, and cut my forehead. The last had taken most of the time to deal with as there was a lot of stitching to do.

Most of these injuries were caused by, or were made worse by, the fact that my safety straps were not tight enough. My face had been mucked up by the gunsight bracket.

I was in Ely R.A.F. Hospital, an immense place full mainly of bomber crews, burnt, injured by flak or cannon shell or bullet, or just knocked about like me, only mostly worse.

There was a chap dying in the next bed as I came round from my anaesthetic, and another chap with an arm missing was bowling a tennis ball down the aisle between the beds at a batsman whose face was covered with bandages standing in front of a trolley as a wicket. They were shouting at the tops of their voices and 'Music While You Work' was pouring from a loudspeaker above my head at a cacophonous volume.

Eventually a ward sister came in and halted the cricket good-naturedly. She came in and looked at me as the newest arrival and was very sweet.

'What hurts most?' she asked.

'My back,' I said; and I am sorry to say I began to cry and she touched the only part of my face that could be touched and gave me something that made me go to sleep again. Before I went off the body was removed from the next bed and somebody who was being sick was wheeled in to take his place.

On my second day at Ely I asked for a pencil and paper and wrote to Charlotte in a spidery scrawl: 'Just bruised all over and rather uncomfortable,' I told her. 'I don't suppose I'll be here for very long as I've got nothing that won't heal quickly.'

Somehow she contrived to come the following day, and what a blessed sight she was walking trimly with her nice familiar straight back right down the length of the ward, peering at every face, and then back again. I was helpless as I still had almost no voice. She was about to leave when she looked at my bed again, came closer, and very cleverly concealed the shock she must have experienced. After she left I asked for a mirror. There were firm rules about mirrors for smashed-up chaps. But I got one in the end and I saw at once that I did indeed look very unfamiliar.

A few days later Pilot Officer Lundin came bouncing into the ward, 'as right as rain' as he put it and soon to be back on flying. There would be an investigation, perhaps a court martial. Slowly and fuzzily, because I was still getting a lot of pain, I realised that either the machine or I was to take all the blame and only I could deny it. No investigator would ever be able to show that that Bristol engine had collected a large number of branches *before* it crashed. The engine had packed up at 100 feet while I was carrying out authorised low flying, and Lundin, with very great skill, had saved both our lives. That was his story and it had better be mine, too, though the threat was implied rather than stated.

What chance would I have, as an unqualified sergeant pilot, against the word of a qualified and commissioned instructor? So, this was how it was recorded, verbally and on a written and signed statement, and I felt awful. I felt worse still when Lundin crashed again soon after, this time *killing* his student. And six months later he killed himself.

Before I left Ely, in romantic hospital 'blues' and a wheel-chair, for Littleport convalescent home, I got a letter from Brian. He had heard of my mishap and was very severe about it. 'Didn't I warn you about low flying,' he wrote. 'It is an extremely dangerous practice?' I ruefully pondered over Beverly Hills's remoteness from war, and was to do so many times again as I skimmed over enemy soil at fifty feet.

But Beverly Hills was also as kind and generous as ever, and food parcels continued to arrive right through the war.

I have always had a talent for getting myself into false positions. London was full of heroes and Charlotte and I used to amuse ourselves counting gallantry ribbons at night clubs, a V.C. counting ten. All I had done so far was to learn to fly, rather slowly and luxuriously, and suffer the misfortune of being injured by a fool. But the embarrassing old hero business came up again when I was on sick leave in London because, I suppose, it could be assumed that my rather curious face had been bashed about by the Hun rather than a gunsight bracket in a trainer I hadn't even been flying at the time.

I tried pulling my forage cap low over my nasty looking forehead and doing without a stick. But all to no avail. Aged bus conductors offered me their frail arms to help me on and off. People yielded their place in cinema queues. Shop assistants asked me in a soft voice how I was feeling. At Keith Prowse in Coventry Street, trying out records, a fabulously famous blonde lady crooner stroked my face and whispered that I ought to go home with her. And so on.

Actually, I wasn't fit to go home with anyone, getting tired very easily and being sick rather a lot when I was. So, one way and another, I was for once glad to get away from London and onto a very soft job in a control tower until my sogginess and dizziness disappeared.

I was flying again in October, warily and with half an eye on that offensive gunsight. In order to do so I had to have new flying gear, and to get this it was necessary to hand in the old stuff—and stuff it was: a shapeless bit of leather stiff with congealed blood and identifiable as a helmet only by the smashed goggles attached to it; an equally unpleasant outer flying suit; and slashed-about gauntlets.

The tarty little W.A.A.F. in stores received them across the counter without comment, or even a glance at me, and dropped them in a box. She returned from the racks in less than a minute, plonking the new gear down still without a word and returning her attention to the *Daily Mirror* and her ciggy butt. No blonde crooner she. Just blasé.

What a long time it took to train a pilot! In the Kaiser War it was a matter of weeks and you could be on a squadron after 20 hours and dead an hour later. Flying, fighting and the machines themselves had become more complicated since then. A year after that first session of aerobatics with my goddamit American crop-duster, I still had the full Operational Training course in front of me.

The same finger of fate that pointed to California with the cry 'Go west, young man', now sent me north and on to single-engine fighters. I didn't ask for them. The only thing I did ask for was night fighters because I liked flying in the dark and fancied the independence of the work. Stalking the foe by moonlight, flitting in and out of the clouds. That kind of thing. I never became a night fighter pilot though I came close to being made to tow target drogues for air gunners to shoot at, and glider towing, and being sent out to India to fly something or other.

It was to be Hurricanes in Scotland, and I surveyed R.A.F. Station Annan with an eye that was becoming wily and discerning. It looked promising, I thought, friendly, busy and enterprising. There was a good man in charge, a Wing Commander David, and I had a first-class Flight Commander, a very civilised Irishman.

Annan was also a dump. Several dozen Nissen and wooden huts had been dumped down on a Scottish hilltop, linked by muddy tracks which wound round the crude dwellings of crofters, who continued somehow to follow their calling amidst the hurly-burly of a thousand airmen and W.A.A.F.s going about their business. We had heavy, fat-tyred bicycles to get from place to place in this sprawling camp, and survived the unspeakable late autumn and winter weather by fighting for a place by the coke stoves.

The wash-houses were as distant as everything else and little used. Indoors and out everyone wore as many clothes as they could lay their hands on, and R.A.F. uniforms were often concealed beneath layers of sweaters and scarves. Sulphurous fumes, the stench of cigarettes and unwashed bodies filled every hut and mess. There was a great deal of cursing and filthy anecdotage, but the talk was otherwise all of flying. Like Watton, this was a hard, professional flying school, and we worked long hours and flew in the foulest weather.

I don't know how many hundreds of pilots were killed at Annan. The total must have been savagely high, though. It was a silly place to have a flying school at all, for Dumfriesshire is not noted for its cloud-free skies. On the contrary, the clouds hang about the hills the year round, and there are higher mountains not far away, north and south.

The airfield itself lay below the living quarters, in a shallow dip, which made the approach tricky for novices under certain conditions. Martin Rivers from school had been killed here, and I looked up the report on his crash in an alarming pile of similar reports. He had flown into a mountain in cloud. Of the twenty on my course, two did the same thing and three others were also killed, too. 25% fatalities was about average.

The dear old Hurricane could not be blamed for this state of affairs. She never let you down. We had about fifty Mark Is, the sort with eight machine-guns, which had accounted for four in five German aircraft shot down by fighters in the Battle of Britain.

There was something about walking out to a Hurricane for the first time that put a jauntiness into your step. You had arrived, you told yourself, you were a man at last. On with that well-worn helmet and oil-stained veteran's Mae West and scramble for those 150 bandits at angels 15.

Although much roomier than a Spitfire's cockpit, a Hurricane's felt claustrophobic and cramped at first. The absence of not only another chap, but another seat for another chap, was at first upsetting, too. Now, decidedly, one was on one's own, so one had better get good at it, hadn't one? Or so I told myself, and in fact for the next nine weeks I worked harder and with greater concentration than at any time in my life.

In pouring rain and low cloud and occasional clear days, by day and by night, we flew, flew, flew—flew formation by the hour, flew as low as we could go, flew as high as we could go—about 35,000 feet—flew mock dogfights, flew aerobatics and flew long distances by compass alone and flew at night above and below cloud.

If there was a day when the fog was down and even the Solway Firth seagulls skulked on the mud, we flew twice as much the next day, perhaps four trips of over an hour, and an hour's night flying at the end. After my weeks in hospital I still got very tired and my left leg ached, especially when flying in formation. But the Hurricane claimed me and I surrendered to its power and its charms that winter.

It was already an obsolete plane and had been too slow for the Battle of Britain. But it was all very much more muscular than playing about with silver 'ships' over the Mojave Desert. With those Browning machine-guns in the wings and that 1,200 hp Rolls-Royce engine up front, I revelled in diving down at 350 mph on a fellow pilot, reflector sight on, safety catch off, twisting and turning to 'get a bead' on the hunch-backed fuselage a hundred yards away. Just the same, it was only film we shot at first and you had to wait until it had been developed to see who had shot down who.

But firing live followed. It was just as everyone had described it and written about it—the machine shuddered with pleasure, the sound was satisfactorily concussive, and when you saw the tracers tearing into the target—even though it was only a canvas drogue—it filled you with a sort of wickedly atavistic glee. Ho, ho! you exclaimed. Fill him full of lead! And the heady smell of cordite filtered into the cockpit.

It was all so simple, just pressing lightly a bakelite button, so clinical and so satisfactory in its results. No wonder people killed with guns. They haven't always been efficient, but they have always demanded so little of the trigger-puller. Now if we had been told to fight for our lives with knives there might have been less talk of 'probables' and 'kills'.

Actually it was very difficult to hit that towed canvas sleeve, 20 feet by 4 feet, doing about 150 mph. You normally came in from behind and a bit above and at about 45 degrees, closing to 100 yards and nerving yourself to get closer still, allowing just the right deflection, keeping the Hurricane's nose steady, remembering to give short bursts.

Now I began to understand why the great majority of fighter pilots went through the Battle of Britain without ever hitting the enemy. We had the advantage of a slow moving, steady target that was not firing back at you, and of my first 600 rounds fewer than 50 went into the drogue. I got this up to about 10%, but that was not a fierce enough threat to the Hun, I thought, and I banged away at the clay pigeon range day after day to try to make the figure more respectable. I stopped at 11.1%. Imagine trying to do it in the *dark*!

But flying the Hurricane at night was a heady, full-blooded experience which did much to flush away my boyhood timorousness and helped to build up the sort of self-confidence I would soon be needing. Whatever the conditions and circumstances, it was a magical business to take this husky machine, exhausts glowing a reassuring blue, up, up to 20,000 feet. On a moonlit night the serrated coast of south-west Scotland, the deep cut of the Solway Firth, the bulge of Cumberland ending at Morecambe Bay, all clearly marked the frontier of black land against the deep mauve of the sea. The fells of Cumbria shimmered white, the lakes were black and sinister below the peaks.

One moonlight night, in an ecstasy of power and joy, I dived my Hurricane vertically towards these mountains from a great height, pulling up low over the Scafell range with throttle wide open. For a few seconds I held the machine upside down at the top of the loop, looking down possessively at this black and white living map. As a boy, every peak had taken sweat out of me. For a moment I owned them all and I was so buoyant with pride that the straps hardly had to hold me. Then I put down the nose again and skimmed Bassenthwaite Lake flat out, weaving from shoreline to shoreline, and so home to bed.

Black nights were harder, especially when there was a lot of cloud about. There wasn't much opportunity for lyrical sentiment in dirty weather at night. At first it was all concentration and fighting off panic. The horizon could be so dim that I would slide open the cockpit canopy, letting in a freezing blast, in order to get a clearer view.

Carlisle always showed a few lights and no one had yet learned how to dim out the funnel glow of steam trains. Pilots had been known to follow the west coast route out of Carlisle to

Dumfries in order to find Annan on the way. At low altitude a car's wartime-dimmed headlights reflected faintly off the road, especially in rain.

At the very start of my training it had all been 'Fly by your goddam ass, Hough, goddam it.' But once off Stearmans the ass was no longer enough, however goddam sensitive it might be. Life soon became too fast and complicated, until it was a mainly useless bit of anatomy at 10,000 feet in thick winter cloud over the Scottish hills.

Faith was what counted now. Spiritual faith, yes. That could be useful. But firm uncompromising faith in your instruments was vital. That was one reason why we spent many hours in Link trainers, those comic dummy cockpits, black as pitch within, pretending to be aeroplanes in dirty weather. They had all the blind flying and other instruments and an aircraft's controls. You took off, gained height, banked and turned, set course, all by instruments, all in perfect safety.

Sometimes your real instruments lied through their teeth. Of course you were straight and level. Your ass and your long experience told you that you were. Take no notice. This damn plane hasn't been properly serviced. Then out of the cloud you came, on your side and in a steep dive, straight for the side of Shap fells. Upsetting.

'Today we're starting on dummy rhubarbs,' our Flight Commander informed us.

'Dummy what?'

'A rhubarb is a low level attack against unspecified targets.'

'You mean a free-for-all rampage?'

'Something like that. But make your targets useful ones. Barracks if you can find any, power stations, ships, docks, trains, that sort of thing. The area has been warned.'

This sounded an amusing diversion. In at nought feet, the Solway being the English Channel, Cumberland France. What those poor people of north Cumberland put up with, year in, year out!

The smooth waters of the Firth slid by just beneath the wings and the low flat coastline raced towards me. The tiniest touch of the stick to clear the marshes and the first hedge. And at that delicate moment practice became reality and the sky was full of tracer, all arching towards me, and I heard the crump of exploding shells and saw the grey cloud puffs ahead and on both sides.

I raced on, unscathed and thoughtful. They did this sort of thing at Army assault courses, but I had never heard of it in R.A.F. flying exercises. It also seemed 'a bit dicey' and might lead to 'a wizard prang'.

Rather cross and fussed I made some especially determined ciné gun attacks against various unfortunate and innocent targets, including a coaster on the way back, and caught glimpses of crouching figures on locomotive footplates, outside a colliery at Whitehaven and on the ship's bridge.

Two others who had followed me had also escaped being hit. It was probably good for us to be blooded in this way, and to give us early warning in our training that our own anti-aircraft gunners were slightly more dangerous than those of the enemy because their behaviour was unpredictable.

A more distant and testing rhubarb target was the Isle of Man. At nought feet a coastline remains concealed until you are almost on top of it, so we had to become skilled not only at skimming the wave tops but also at steering a compass course accurately at the same time. Normally we affected to despise compass navigation, priding ourselves on our map-reading abilities. When it was pointed out to us that within a few weeks our accuracy would determine whether we hit the enemy coast between, or on top of, German anti-aircraft batteries, we tried very hard indeed.

In fact life at this time was becoming altogether too intense and serious for my taste. Nor did Christmas add much gaiety to the scene. No one in the services was allowed to travel by rail between 20th and 28th December, which led to bitter comment, and every barracks and station throughout the land had to lay on its own entertainment.

Apart from bringing in the odd band and comedian, this consisted mainly of free beer and more food than usual, and visiting and being visited, all in an ever-increasing state of drunkenness—airmen's mess to sergeants' mess, the sergeants to officers' mess, the local A.T.S. to the airmen's dance, a detachment of sailors to the W.A.A.F.s' mess, soldiers to a sing-song in the sergeants' mess, and so on, all more and more noisily until the first fighting and vomiting.

This encouragement of egalitarianism, so well intentioned, always led to trouble. Deprived of their class and income jealousies, their boss and worker conflicts, then inter-service and inter-rank warfare hotted up. The Army and the Navy loathed the R.A.F. because of its spurious glamour and adulation gained during the Battle of Britain, and assisted by the biggest and best public relations department of all the services.

The Army could not forgive itself for pulling out of Dunkirk. The R.A.F. could never forgive the Navy for being socially superior. And so on. In the lower echelons the Army could never forgive its own A.T.S. girls for despising them and going for the Navy or the Brylcreem Boys, and made up for it by going hell for leather for any W.A.A.F. they could lay their hands on, and there were plenty of them, thank goodness.

Christmas boredom and Christmas booze brought out the worst in everyone. A mildly embarrassing midday Christmas dinner at which the officers waited on the non-commissioned officers, and the sergeants on the men, deteriorated during the afternoon and evening until the first boozy fighting broke out.

Too self-conscious to be a good joiner-in, and a bit 'pi' in those days, too, the whole thing filled me with horror. I wrote home that Christmas had 'induced in me a sense of gloom, and finally retreated to bed when I saw a girl being sick in the middle of the floor.'

However, the last of my training ended on a high note. The fun came in the air rather than on the ground, which was only right and proper. I had nearly 350 hours in my logbook and felt a complete happiness with the Hurricane, a happiness that I discovered with no other fighting aircraft. I had mastered it, and we were friends, like a good man-and-working-dog relationship. Its power, particularly in the climb, was limited, but it allowed you to take every sort of liberty without hitting back, was marvellously responsive and manoeuvrable, as many a Messerschmitt pilot had already discovered, was tough and could take a beating, and was still fast enough to be fun.

I found a friend, a Pilot Officer, on the last stage of operational training at the satellite airfield of Longtown near Carlisle. He felt the same about the Hurricane as I did and was exactly my standard as a pilot. We flew together for hours over the border counties, revelling in our skill and competitiveness, taking off in formation, climbing as if tied wingtip to wingtip by a short length of string, and doing evolutions together, first one and then the other leading.

I was never to taste flying like this again, with all the joys of a wonderful single-seat fighter and none of the worries of combat. For no special reason we roared with laughter at one another at 20,000 feet above the earth and 35 feet from each other, slid open our hoods and took off our masks to grimace and pretend we didn't need oxygen. Then we clipped them back on again and called out 'O.K.' on the radio. We broke apart and engaged in furious dogfighting for half an hour at a time, dodging in and out of cloud, holding each other's tail through rolls and loops and Immelmanns until we were both utterly exhausted.

We never shot one another down with our ciné cameras, and we wondered if that was a good or a bad omen for the future. On the ground we played chess when we weren't talking flying. Our friendship was built round the Hawker Hurricane, the love for which we shared with a growing passion as the last

84

days of the course drew near and we thought it was unlikely that we would ever fly her again.

We were rightly warned of over-confidence by our Flight Commander. As consolation, we were graded joint top on our course. But I think this was based on our showing over the last weeks when nothing seemed to go wrong and we were driven on by Jupiter himself.

During the last days of 1942 we were sent off to different single-seat fighter squadrons and never saw or heard of one another again. It was typical of service friendships. His name was Johnny Hadow. I hope he survived.

5

I stood on an exposed wooden station platform in a cold January wind with a kitbag, a parachute bag and a suitcase, greatcollar turned up, waiting for transport. Half service life was spent waiting for a Bedford lorry and a hard swearing W.A.A.F. driver at the wheel with a ciggy stuck to her lower lip. But she and her rattley, camouflage-painted Bedford were more welcome at a winter wayside halt even than Kay Francis's chauffeur and Packard sliding up to the Little Mocambo at 3 a.m.

For a period of stalemate in the war, it was incredible how everyone seemed to be travelling from one place to another and for no apparent purpose. 'Is Your Journey Really Necessary?' screamed a poster at me. And, yes it was, I responded jauntily. I've got a posting to a hush-hush squadron—and that's ace gen. So, fair enough, let's get crackin'—it's the real thing at last. Wizzo!

And I should think so too. It was eighteen months since I'd been checked for V.D. at Lords, twelve since Hollywood had opened her scented arms to me.

Very early that morning I had said good-bye to my parents at Brighton, where they sat out the war as they had sat out the Kaiser War, enduring the civilian rigours stoically, flinching away from the horrors, their pacifist principles in confusion. They did not know quite what to do about me either, and I was sorry for them, and for defecting from them even before the war had swallowed me up. I think I made them uneasy, and I was certainly uneasy with them. They preferred to be with my elder brother who was more comprehensible and less irritating and had chosen to be a farmer.

'Where are you off to now, son?' asked my father from his bed. He was wearing two thick sweaters on top of his pyjamas and was settling down to his first big cup of tea when I came in at half past six. He was reading Shaw's *Fabian Essays* which he annotated in pencil in the margin in his steep-sloping spidery hand. We had played chess the evening before and for the first time in my life I had beaten him level. He had felt it very badly, but nothing like as badly as I had. If *only* I had let him take my rook!

'I'm going on a squadron.'

'Where will you be, abroad?'

'Some rather remote place in Yorkshire. Hutton Cranswick. I can't tell you what I'm flying because that's secret. I expect you'll read about them soon, though.'

'Look after yourself, son.' He gave me a good hard grip. When I got to the door and turned, the pencil was already in action.

It was only half past three in the afternoon when the train had arrived at Hutton Cranswick, but it was already twilight. There was a sound in the air above the station platform. It had a deep note and was quite unfamiliar. We were experienced in the sounds of all R.A.F. machines now, as we were in their shapes. But here in the grey Yorkshire sky was a new shape and a new sound.

A section of four Typhoons roared overhead at a thousand feet—and a heart which I flattered myself was now hard and cynical beat a great deal faster. They looked like heavy-jawed, pugnacious Hurricanes, with strongly canted, thick wings from which sprouted four 20 mm. cannon.

The four machines spread out and dropped their wide

undercarriages, radiator flaps, wing flaps and tail wheels together. As the leader turned for his landing run his Typhoon took on the guise of an aggressive, crouching predator poised to leap on its foe. Seven tons, I had been told. 412 mph straight and level! I was expected to fly *that*! Not only fly it but fight in it! Impossible, utterly ludicrous.

There was a hoot behind me and I turned. Transport had arrived. A little Commer with, for once, a rather pretty driver. I straightened my back, threw the kitbag over my shoulder, and marched smiling to meet my doom.

My driver's laconic speech and professionalism at the wheel matched the whole style of my first operational airfield. Everything about Hutton Cranswick was brisk and matter-of-fact. Here no one felt impelled to make their mark and prove themselves. It was assumed that you were a pro, and that was very refreshing—not poor Lundin's scene at all.

All through the long training your standing was governed by the petty snobberies of experience. 'Get some in!' jeered the cadets in their new uniforms in St John's Wood at those who arrived in civvies a week after them. Getting time in was a status activity I never understood. The ultimate élite were those with a second class aircraftsman's rank and three long service stripes—hinting at periods in the glasshouse and frequent demotion—rather than an airman who shot to the top of the non-commissioned ranks through merit and enthusiasm. There were no old lags like service old lags.

Being 'on ops' was a wonderful leveller, just as there is no room for small snobberies in any front line.

'What else have you got besides Typhoons?' I asked my pretty driver with the nicotine-stained fingers.

'Spits,' she said, swinging in through the main gates and throwing a kiss to the guard. 'Poles. Mad as hatters.' There was a pause. 'You're for 195?'

'Yup.'

'God help you.'

88

9 Flak over a convoy off the Dutch coast between Den Helder and Texel, August 1943. The Beaufighters blew up a minesweeper.

10a/b Landing after hectic Rhine crossing operations in March 1945.

11 As a scruffy Flight-Lieutenant about to go off blasting a German Paratroop Brigade H.Q., late April 1945, armed with two 500-pounders, four 20 mm. cannon and a .38 Smith and Wesson in case of further difficulty.
(*Inset*) Our first daughter's first birthday.

12a Parachute Brigade H.Q. near Oldenburg after 197 Squadron had dealt with it with 500-pounder delayed action bombs. I went back and took this a few hours later.

12b German ground fire remained lethal right to the end of the war. Fellow pilot is Bobby Farmiloe.

13a/b Military store near Oldenburg dive-bombed by 197 Squadron with 500 pounders. (*Above*) This was how it looked six hours later, and (*below*) a month later on the advance through Germany when we examined our handiwork from ground level. The army felled the chimney for safety reasons. Four of us (*centre*) argue about whose hole is who's!

14 Forward airstrip, Mill, Holland.

15a With 24 cylinders, sleeve valves, 2-stage supercharger, and two-and-a-half thousand horsepower, the Tiffy's Sabre engine was a fitter's nightmare.

15b Rearming with 20 mm. cannon shells after a straffing raid.

16a/b As we moved up through Germany during the last stage of the war we found ourselves sharing airfields with our old antagonists like the Heinkel 219 (*below*) and the long-nose Focke-Wulf 190 and Messerschmitt Me 110.

195 was a new squadron, not yet fully worked up for operations, commanded by a Battle of Britain pilot, Don 'Butch' Taylor. He was a ginger-haired chap, very bouncy and jokey, a cheerful soul and a good pilot. Most of the pilots were new to squadron life, a mixed lot as usual, from randy and boozy and coarse-tongued to reasonably well educated. I especially liked Johnny Webster, from Stowe and trained in California, too. Like me, he had not put in for a commission, because he preferred the cheapness and egalitarianism of the sergeants' mess, though we both changed our minds later and applied.

The Poles looked very foreign and very gentlemanly beside the 195 lot, who wore old sweaters and filthy trousers and oil-stained silk scarves and shaved every other day. The Poles looked elegant and did not sprawl as we did, but their dark Slav passions broke out suddenly, without warning, in the bar usually very late at night. And then there was much breaking of furniture.

In their Spitfires they were peerlessly efficient, blindly brave and absolutely dedicated killers. They had blown up two Messerschmitt Bf 109s that morning—and I mean blown up, for they would follow them down even when the pilot was dead and his machine on fire, banging away at them; and would continue to do so after they crashed if they had the chance.

The Poles' hatred of the German was hair-raising. To each other, and to us, their manner was courtly and elegant. But they did not bother to learn English. It suited them not to understand British controllers on the R/T who would certainly attempt to stem their enthusiasm to get at the enemy. We liked and respected them, and were devoutly thankful that they were on our side.

My Flight Commander, a rather stiff, elderly regular called Jonson, ordered me to the dispersal after lunch and gave me a run-down on the Typhoon. 'We've only had them a few weeks and they can be sods. They're also bloody fast—make rings round the 190. Sink like a stone if you have to ditch.'

I had already learned a bit about the secret 'Tiffy' at O.T.U. After Sydney Camm had got the Hurricane into production in 1937, he was already thinking of its successor. Camm believed in strength and durability in his fighters. The Hurricane could take damage which would cause a Spitfire to fall to pieces. He also had his eye on a Napier engine rather than a Rolls-Royce—a very remarkable and complex engine designed by Frank Holford. This was the sleeve-valve, 24-cylinder (in horizontal 'H' form), two-stage-supercharged Sabre, perhaps the most brilliant and certainly the most powerful piston aircraft engine of all time.

The crises of Munich and May 1940 put back development of this new fighter while all resources were concentrated on producing the established Spitfire and Hurricane. It was rumoured Rolls-Royce did not fancy this threat to their monopoly with the Merlin. If that was the case someone ought to have been shot, for, soon after the Battle of Britain, there developed an urgent need for a much faster British fighter to combat the Focke-Wulf 190.

The consequence was that the Typhoon was hustled into production long before it had been properly tested let alone developed to service standards. As one historian has written, 'The circumstances surrounding the Typhoon's entry into the R.A.F. can only be described as macabre. Had such events occurred in peacetime they would most certainly have been the subject of searching questions in Parliament. But this was war and the enemy possessed an aircraft . . . that posed a serious barrier to Britain's determination to win air superiority over France and the Low Countries.'

The engine was a knock-out but at this time appallingly unreliable. The airframe had not been fully tested and tails fell off with disquieting frequency. Other Typhoons disappeared less spectacularly but more mysteriously, and it was only after some time and a number of losses that it was discovered that carbon monoxide filtered back into the cockpit.

From then, until the last time I flew them in July 1945, we wore oxygen masks even when running up on the ground.

This Sabre engine was also inclined to catch fire on starting, and starting drill included a specially appointed fitter holding a fire extinguisher at the ready. Spitfire pilots were always astonished at this evidence of imminent catastrophe. 'You get used to everything and it only happens sometimes,' we would reply.

There was also some delay in the supply of Hispano cannon so that many early Typhoons carried only machine-guns. And it was little consolation to a Typhoon pilot that he had no fewer than twelve of these .303 Brownings set into his wings when they were all outranged and every bullet non-explosive. I often flew the 12-gun Typhoon. Once I was lucky with my drogue shooting and the canvas was torn to shreds before my eyes. But even two cannon would have been better.

However, by the time I arrived at 195 they were strengthening the tail by the simple process of riveting fishplates all round the suspect area, the engines were reputed to be somewhat more reliable, and no more 12-gun Tiffies were sent to us.

'There's a lot of crap talked about the Tiffy,' said Jonson reassuringly but within the sound of a distinctly off-tune engine being run up, cowling removed, by a group of oily-overalled fitters.

Then he gave me ground drill in the Typhoon's cockpit. From time to time in the 1970s I look in at the Imperial War Museum where they have a Typhoon's cockpit standing rather forlornly without engine or airframe, and a short flight of steps from which you can peer through the perspex into the mysteries of the interior. And mysteries they are to me today, although if I look long enough a dim memory of the function of this or that knob and lever and dial filters back mistily through the decades.

There was a real man's throttle handle, rather like one of the old lift controls in Harrods, with a 'stop' which you could break through for ultimate boost, so long as you had a good explanation afterwards, and alongside it the mixture control, pitch control for the propeller, and the two-stage supercharger control.

Trim, flaps, Koffman starter, hood release, rad control, undercart lever—it is ridiculous that my fumbling, impractical hands once reached the right one with masterful grasp and activated some mechanical miracle in this elaborate engineering organism upon which my life depended.

There was a letter from Allan Palmer waiting for me in the mess, written from 183 Squadron at Church Fenton. 'Ho, ho!' it began cheerfully, 'fancy you being on Typhoons too! They'll give you a headache or two as they have me—absolute bastards. . . .' Poor Allan was picked off by German flak going in low over the French coast not long after this and before we could meet again.

Like most pilots, I became attached to the Typhoon if only for its uncompromising masculinity. The Spitfire was essentially a feminine machine, dainty, provocative, not always predictable. The Hurricane was all-male, but gentlemanly. To take off a Typhoon was to grapple with a low-bred all-in wrestler, and the thud of the wheels tucking in to the belly after take-off was like the sound of the bell at the end of the round. At first, every take-off, however strenuous, was also a victory; every landing a world war triumph.

I can write with authority about my first proper Typhoon flight—as opposed to some early circuits and bumps with Jonson virtually talking me down—because it is as clearly etched in my mind as that other flight with Lundin some months earlier.

Even to get into the cockpit was like climbing Nape's Needle without ropes. You pulled down one vestigial step from the beast's belly, hauled yourself onto the starboard wing root, grasped the door handle, opened up a spring-loaded crevice in the fuselage for your left foot, dragged open the door with its perspex canopy and window, and with a final breathtaking effort, swung over the sill and down into the seat.

After a short rest, your rigger helped you into your straps, opened your window, closed your door, jumped down, slipped the step back into the belly and stood by the chocks while you went, first, through the arduous cockpit drill and the preparations for bringing the beast alive.

It was in keeping that an explosion was needed to start the Sabre. Like the Smith and Wesson .38 revolver we later carried at our waist, the Koffman had six rounds. You selected one, under the dash, and pulled a bit of wire. There was an explosion, those twenty-four pistons were forced into motion, the three-bladed propeller lurched into circulation, all manner of vapour and smoke issued from the exhausts, the airman with the extinguisher took aim. Then the Sabre subsided into silent sleep again.

Usually after the third or fourth attempt, accompanied by throttle jiggling, the engine burst into activity, the exhaust fumes were coughed away like catarrh, and the whole airframe quivered with eagerness to be off. After running up to check rev fall on the magnetos and a few other processes, you prepared for the ordeal of getting it into the air: full left rudder trim, left foot locked hard on its pedal, throttle lever pushed firmly open, fifteen degrees of flap.

With 2,600 hp behind it, the engine was equally anxious to spin the aircraft as the propeller. The torque was fierce, and even with full left rudder the Typhoon sidled like a petulant stallion determined not to gallop straight. But with this acceleration, that pushed your back hard against the armour-plated seat, the Typhoon was soon in the air.

Then—undercart up, window closed, rad flap up, flaps up at 500 feet, and you could begin to revel in the exuberance of the power.

The Typhoon *was* power. Power was its *raison d'être*. You could do anything with it and it had no special vices in spite of its dark record. It responded obediently and reasonably quickly to your will. But its great weight and its great power were equally and always evident, and in time you learned to exploit these attributes. After the Hurricane it represented a new dimension in flying.

I was ordered off that January morning to do a 'sector recce', which meant do what you like within the regulations, don't go too far, and watch out for the balloons over Hull and elsewhere. South of the Humber I flew out to sea at 3,000 feet. It was a nice clear winter day, I was in the fastest fighter in the world, and I was even beginning to feel that I might one day tame it. So I did a bit of diving and aerobatting around, noting how she dropped like a meteorite if you put the nose down and that you needed to probe the stratosphere before beginning a loop.

Then the engine felt that it had had enough for that day, and stopped. Of course, it was bound to start again when I switched fuel tanks—must have run one too low. Careless fellow. It didn't, and I noted that I was still out to sea and recalled Jonson's comments about ditching.

So I pulled the nose up to bring down the speed to 140 mph and headed for land in the shallowest glide I could manage—and with all that weight it wasn't very shallow. Silence is not golden in a fighter with a dead engine over the sea. It is profoundly upsetting. I continued to pray for the impossible as the low coastline approached, much too slowly. There was a click and a whoosh and then a considerable draught of air when I ejected the canopy. Then I bent over to turn off the fuel, and tightened my straps.

A strong east wind took me miraculously over the marshy Lincolnshire shore a few hundred feet up, and ahead there lay some very comfortingly flat fens, their beauty compromised only by wide drainage ditches.

When I touched earth in the middle of a ploughed field the Typhoon seemed to slide on for ever. Without flaps and with wheels up the stalling speed was well over 100 mph and there was a lot of weight and momentum as well as wind behind me. Mud sprayed up on both sides, a bank made me airborne again, and like a bad steeplechaser at Becher's I went through the next hedge as if it didn't exist, over another ditch and on and on, bumping and tossing about.

'Just when I thought I'd never stop,' I wrote to Charlotte, 'a final jar, followed by eerie silence except for a drip of escaping oil and petrol and the hiss of a very hot engine half in a pool of water.'

I had the straps off in no time and leaped out and raced off as fast as I could go. At a safe distance I sat down on a bank. My long-suffering nose was bruised again and my newly-mended back muscles had taken a beating, but otherwise I was all right. I lit a cigarette and contemplated the ruin—to the farmer and the R.A.F. alike.

It was a simple enough crash landing, but the four-hundred-yard-long slide had cut a deep gouge in the rich Lincolnshire fields, spoiled the symmetry of three banks and a hedge, and cast a long line of aircraft bits into the mud.

I didn't expect this episode to go down in any R.A.F. annals. But it was a bit wounding that no one had seen it happen, nor even acknowledged that I was here, safe on mother earth, after my death-defying performance. All about me, as far as the eye could see, were flat fens with not a dwelling in sight, let alone a human being. Where were those kindly women, with their cups of tea and comforting motherly bosoms who were always there to meet downed fighter chaps? Where was the inevitable village constable? 'Now, what's going on 'ere, Sir? Oh, I see, Sir. A spot of trouble, eh? Did you get a Jerry first, Sir?' That was the sort of reception the Battle of Britain boys got.

Instead, it was a long trudge into the nearest village of Maltby-le-Marsh and the cups of tea and bosoms. The police-man appeared and did his bit, and I sent him off to guard the plane, whispering that it was on the secret list, which instilled a new authority into his stride across the fens. The village schoolmistress broke up the school for the day, and after getting my shaky autograph, off the children excitedly dashed to stare at the ruin from as near as the bobby would let them.

'I've got a nice bit of pork here, sir,' said the pink-cheeked postmistress. A stiffish gin would undoubtedly have gone down better. But the meal was so carefully laid out in the parlour, with a bottle of 'Daddie's Sauce', that I could hardly refuse.

Sabres rattled and coughed and spluttered and even momentarily conked out from time to time after this. But they never actually left me high and dry again, and I soon forgave the Tiffy this rather robust introductory performance, and set about mastering her thoroughly. I never loved her, and mastery was not the right word for a relationship with this remarkable machine. One reached an armed truce, an understanding brought about by a balance of terror, like relations between the great powers after the war that she did her considerable bit towards winning.

My real love on 195 was the squadron Tiger Moth. Everyone else despised this dainty little biplane that made the Stearman seem like a sound-barrier-breaking rocket. But I loved getting into its open rear cockpit, persuading a fitter to give the prop a turn, and then go jogging off across the grass, without even a radio to bother about, and up into the air in a few yards. The Moth brought sanity and simplicity back to flying, for the raging Tiffy was always on the brink of hysteria.

In addition to my normal duties, I became unofficial errand boy. 'Hough, there's a magneto we need badly at Coltishall.' A check on the weather, and off I would go with a map, hugging the shore, free from the disciplines which governed everyday squadron flying. No one minded how low you flew in an inoffensive Moth, and even the anti-aircraft gunners left you alone. Normally I kept at fifty feet, with an occasional cheery hand-wave to landgirls on their tractors. Everyone was your friend in a Moth and you had time for the little courtesies of life.

Once, crossing the Pennines in the teeth of a westerly gale, I kept company with an army convoy on Snake Pass for several miles. When the road straightened out and they began to go downhill I could no longer keep up with them, and the soldiers' cheerful waving turned to jeers.

The only person on 195 who shared my love for the little Moth was the Intelligence Officer, a 'penguin Spy' as they were unhappily termed, Pilot Officer Hugh. Hugh could never have been folded into a Typhoon though he weighed no more than seven stone. Pale of countenance and serious in demeanour, the Spy retained throughout the months I knew him a touching and innocent admiration of us pilots. Every day was another day of awesome wonder that he was being allowed to serve us. Most intelligence officers treated their pilots with amiable scepticism and believed claims only when they were thrice corroborated and backed by a ciné gun film. Hugh seized hold of the smallest hint of damage to the enemy as further proof of the courage and daring of his heroes. He should have served with Captain Ball in Flanders. He would have been busier and less mercilessly teased.

Hugh would sometimes drop hints that the Moth was serviced and refuelled and there wasn't much doing for me for a few hours, and anyway there were some new maps for us at Church Fenton which ought to be collected and he ought to have a word with the senior I.O. there. And off we would go. Hugh sat forward in a borrowed helmet and leather jacket that came nowhere near reaching his waist. I insisted on his bending forward at take-off as his narrow shoulders and long neck obstructed my view.

Once in the air he was also in his seventh heaven. I derived vast satisfaction from the way his head turned constantly from side to side in wonder at the magic of flying, and the way he

97

would point downwards at some farmer's wife hanging out the washing. I would do a tight turn so that he could wave.

When life became more serious, the Spy became the most diligent of I.O.s, and our mockery soon turned to respect. But long before that time, we became friends in our joint love of the dear little de Havilland biplane.

In fact life did not become serious, as we had expected it would, when we moved from Hutton Cranswick to Formby in Lancashire, ostensibly (and ridiculously) to defend Liverpool. Night raids on this battered city had long since ceased and day bombers would have been intercepted before they could have reached this far north. However, the odd German reconnaissance plane came over to spot the arrival and departure of convoys, and we were supposed to nip up and shoot them down before they could return home. We were not high altitude interceptors, the second stage of our superchargers losing efficiency above 20,000 feet.

Formby was a soft station, and Southport nearby was full of rich businessmen and their fat, furred wives who had left their suburban mansions outside blitzed Liverpool and Manchester to sit out the war at the Prince of Wales Hotel. We were very rude to them and they were very rude to us.

But we loved the Lancashire ladies who came out from their factories in coaches to look at the planes they helped to make, and we who flew them. The N.A.A.F.I. brought out endless urns of sweet tea and we sat about and joked with them, and tried to get them into our cockpits but they were too fat and giggly. So one of us would get airborne and show off, grazing the tops of their coaches at 400 mph until they screamed with wonder. Once, as I was clambering out from my cockpit, one of these darlings of around 16 stone pushed a halfcrown down the front of my Mae West as a tearful token of her esteem. I didn't know whether to laugh, or cry with her.

Charlotte came up from London to stay with a great-aunt in Southport. We walked the deserted sand dunes during off-duty periods watching the birds, and the Tiffies taking off over our heads, tucking in their wheels just above us. We decided to get married as soon as possible, just in case. She was going into the W.R.N.S. and she would never get leave at the same time as me unless we were married. Most flight commanders didn't approve of marriage. But Jonson had been married for years and didn't mind. He even told me I ought to put in for a commission, cheerfully adding that the widow's pension was much better.

By April we were expecting to move down south any day. We were now fully operational and worked well together. Nor did the Typhoon care for the Formby sand, which got into the Sabre's sleeve valves. It was ludicrous that we should be wasting our power and speed up here when the south and east coast towns were being daily tip-and-run bombed by Focke-Wulf 190s which the Spits couldn't catch. My home town of Brighton was suffering frequently at this time. A lot of people were being killed and morale was suffering.

The call came suddenly on 13 May. There was far too much joking as we packed everything up in a rush, and the C.O. and Flight Commanders became ratty in their effort to show they were business-like rather than fussed. This time I refused the Moth. You could not arrive decently in a battle zone in a Tiger Moth—I mean, you would look very un-Captain Ballish. So I rather regretfully allowed the Spy to be transported by a new lad who had just joined us and took off in my favourite Tiffy with the rest.

We rarely flew as a complete squadron, partly because we rarely had twelve serviceable aircraft. But that morning we had fourteen and we made an impressive picture of power as we formed up over Southport and then flew low over the hotels, hoping that we would force some of those dyed-blonde-and-corseted ladies to duck under the bar with their lunchtime martinis.

Then we set course south-east at a steady economical

cruising speed of 280 mph for East Anglia. Our destination was a Coltishall satellite airfield, Ludham, among the Norfolk Broads and the nearest English airfield to Germany. The Luftwaffe was constantly beating up the Norfolk and Suffolk ports and coastal towns, slipping away at nought feet over the North Sea before the Mark V Spitfires were even airborne. Most Typhoon squadrons were now dealing effectively with the same problem in Kent and Sussex. East Anglia was to be our responsibility.

The Americans had arrived in strength since I had last flown about Norfolk, and the whole of East Anglia looked more than ever like an unsinkable aircraft carrier, with the circuit of one airfield almost overlapping its neighbour's. By the time we reached Norwich we had seen not only hundreds of Bomber Command Lancasters and Halifaxes on the ground, and old friends like Beaufighters and Spitfires, but also more unfamiliar shapes of American Bostons and Flying Fortresses and even the bizarre twin-boom form of P38 Lightning escort fighters, which I had first noted in California skies more than a year ago.

'Round the clock' bombing of Germany was getting under way. But our concern, as the fastest machines in East Anglia, was the defence of towns against German fighter-bombers.

Ludham was a nice, small, informal airfield, and it was pleasant at last not to have to share with anyone else. There was much jovial drinking in the mess that first night, and my mind went back twelve months to that last jolly week-end with Brian and Joan. 'This time a year ago,' I mentioned injudiciously, 'I had Claire Trevor in my arms and we murmured how much we loved each other.'

This was a conversation-stopper. Someone threw some beer in my face. 'And I did loops over Ginger Rogers's house and promised Ronald Colman I'd shoot down lots of Huns for him. . . .'

'Pack of lies . . .' 'Hough line-shooting again . . .' 'Get his bags off . . .' They attacked me and I bought drinks all round.

Not one single soul had been known to believe my Hollywood glam tales. That night I consoled myself thinking of Ginger before I went rather dizzily to sleep and dreamed of Messerschmitts falling out of the sky. Perhaps at long last it *would* be the real thing and I would never again have to hang my head in shame and slink away from that milk bar. . . .

We were given twenty-four hours to settle in, become fully operational and learn the sector we would be working in. 'It's going to be bloody boring,' Don Taylor warned us, 'and I don't know how the erks are going to cope. But we'll be on standing patrol in pairs, up and down the coast, Southwold to Yarmouth, all through daylight hours. 1,000 feet—and don't go to bloody sleep.'

'Could I have an early one, please sir?' I asked.

'Why?' he barked. I had done something to displease him but did not know what.

'It's my twenty-first birthday and I'm going to have a party.'

Taylor did not say anything, but when the roster went up I saw I was flying in the morning and on the last patrol in the evening, which with double British summer time in mid-May effectively finished any idea of a celebration.

Taylor had appointed himself as my leader in the evening and I gave him a single glance of hostility when we met at the dispersal hut and silently donned Mae Wests and helmets and parachutes.

'Where are your gauntlets?' he demanded tersely.

The Typhoon was a hot plane with all that engine in front of you and we often flew in shirt sleeves. But leather gauntlets, as protection against burnt hands which might prevent your jettisoning the hood or pulling your ripcord, were *de rigueur*.

'Keep your eyes open,' he shouted at me before starting his engine.

We took off in loose formation and were at the coast in a couple of minutes, picking up the two we were relieving a mile out to sea. Radio silence was rigidly enforced, but they waggled their wings in greeting and sped home to the mess bar at which I should now be presiding. What a way to spend your 21st— up and down, up and down! You could hardly see a thing anyway. The sun had already set and it would be almost pitch dark at the end of our 1½-hour stint.

There was no visible moon, and halfway through the patrol flying south off Lowestoft you could hardly distinguish the blackness of the towns against either land or sea. The sea front was suddenly a mass of sparkles, broken by the bright yellow splashes of exploding bombs. At the same time my headphones were almost blown off by a hysterical jabbering which included repeatedly the word 'bandits'—the code word for enemy aircraft.

I broke radio silence and transmitted, 'Calm down and give us the gen!' But my appeal was lost in the hysteria of other voices screaming from sector control and radar stations. I looked across at Taylor, a dozen wingspans away on my port side. He had begun weaving, searching for some sign of the foe in the dusk, and we had both instinctively opened wide our throttles.

The only clue to the enemy's progress down the coast was the flash of anti-aircraft guns and the spasmodic eruption of a bomb blast. Approaching Southwold, as innocent and pretty a coastal village as you could find in all East Anglia, we had still seen no sign of an aircraft. There were flashes in the village as bombs exploded, killing a dozen more people in houses near the church, I later learned.

I knew that the only chance of catching sight of the dark shapes of the planes was against the lighter background of the sea. And they would have to turn for home soon.

Sure enough, like frightened fish, a string of single-engined fighters poured out of the Southwold area ahead at nought feet, going so fast that my first thought was 'We can never catch *them*!' I gave up counting at fifteen and tried to shout a warning to Taylor but the ether was still jammed with the ludicrous shrill voice of the panicky controller.

Taylor appeared to have seen nothing. But surely he would notice me going down, and if we delayed another second we would lose the lot.

Ah, if Ronald Colman and Ginger Rogers could see me now! Captain Ball of 195 taking on impossible odds, slipping the safety catch off the gun button, speeding down on the Red Baron's tail.

From 500 feet I watched what I thought was the last of the Huns leaving the coast. They were Messerschmitts—Bf 109Fs. I switched on my reflector sight, but it wasn't working properly. It either shone full on, or full off. No dim. This was a singular disadvantage under these almost black conditions.

Furious and thoroughly fussed, I closed up hard astern of my victim, having no trouble at all in matching his speed at three-quarter throttle. I tried firing both ways—first without a sight at all, and then blinded by it. To my surprise a few bits fell off and flashed towards me in his slipstream. He began defensively jigging sharply up and down, something we couldn't do with our carburetters but which the fuel-injected Daimler-Benz engine could take. The one directly in front of him was as likely to be receiving my half-blind fire as my primary target, and might have been for all I knew as I hosed away for all I was worth.

More by luck than anything else enough of my cannon shells were biting home because I dimly perceived more and more bits breaking loose. Then there was a huge splash and I saw something large and dark bouncing off the water, then another spread of white spume. I don't think I had done for two Huns; I think it was the same 109 bouncing twice, but I may have been over-conservative in my claim.*

A moment earlier in this weird game of blind man's buff I

*As this was going to press I checked the official history for the first time and it says there were 26 109s, two being shot down.

had seen shells spattering the sea at about forty-five degrees from my line of flight and for a moment I had thought my shooting was more atrocious than even I had judged it to be. Now I was suddenly aware that it might not be my shooting at all. It might be someone else's—like Don Taylor's by mistake. Anything could happen in this light.

At the same time I was aware of a certain instability in my hard-pressed Tiffy and judged it time to be hauling out of line. As I climbed and turned back towards the coast again, I glanced behind me and was deeply affronted—that is the right word— to see a sparkle of muzzle flashes from many guns pointing at *me*!

It couldn't be the enemy, I told myself innocently. It *must* be my commanding officer, and I flashed the letter of the day— long, long, short, long—on my fuselage light. That didn't do any good. The offensive fire continued, and I had no ammunition left. So I put my game machine on its tail and left it to the Sabre to take me away from this unpleasant chap. Never were its 2,600 horses to be so handy.

As I crossed the coast the batteries gave me their customary going over but they could no more hit me than 15 Huns in a row, and as I steered for home in almost pitch blackness I was able to contemplate my wings and muse that the Captain Ball description 'Shot through and through like a colander' was quite apt for this condition.

But some of my faculties were still functioning, including the radio. 'Put some bloody lights on—please,' I called out, 'and have the bloody blood wagon out.'

I was half cross and half elated but felt better when the wheels came down and locked. No flaps, but never mind. I throttled back, keeping the stick hard over to offset the drag from a large sheet of torn metal sticking up from the port wing, and came over the trees at the end of the east-west runway at a rush. I needed all that length of runway to drag myself to a standstill, and more would have been welcome. There was a nasty smell of burning rubber hanging about in the night air when I turned off onto the perimeter track and taxied past the control tower.

The whole squadron was at the dispersal, except for two who had been scrambled much too late and had not yet returned. Taylor was among those who crowded round me. So it *was* a Hun firing at me, and my victim had *not* been the last out from the coast. Taylor had seen absolutely nothing and had returned home very cross indeed, although he was pleased about me and said so.

After I was chaired to the dispersal someone got out a torch and we all went round the stout Tiffy together counting holes. We gave up at twenty machine gun and six cannon cavities, the latter alarmingly large. Why only the flap controls had suffered beggared imagination, but it made everyone feel much more confidence in this maligned beast.

The dear Spy was in such a state of shattered excitement that he could hardly write out his report and kept demanding repeat descriptions of what he regarded as the most heroic episode in flying since Lindbergh's Atlantic exploit. Later I heard him on the telephone to Group as I left the Flight Office, and his own rendering of the affair was like one of the more lurid passages from a Captain Johns 'Biggles' book.

In the end, therefore, I had an even bigger 21st party than I had planned as all the officers came to the Sergeants' Mess, too, and I was made to drink an enormous vase full of warm bitter beer. Then I was made to send telegrams to Charlotte and my parents, and received a message of congratulation from the A.O.C. 12 Group.

I went to bed even more blearily than I had exactly twelve months earlier after I had lived it up on the Sunset Strip instead of the North Sea.

On hangover morning, 16 May 1943, I was given a nice new Typhoon, 'G' for Georgina. The rigger painted the letters on the nose, and he added a discreet swastika alongside. Georgina was a nice Typhoon, and she saw me safely all through the busy summer of 1943.

The days were long and hot at Ludham. The standing patrols, and that late night Saturday scrap in which they had suffered surprise and damage, had finished German tip-and-running, though we did not yet know it. After three weeks of standing patrols we were down to five serviceable aircraft out of seventeen, the Sabre engine at that time requiring a major overhaul after a mere eight flying hours. Group therefore put us on instant readiness instead, which meant that we sat in pairs at the end of the runway awaiting the red light of a Very pistol and the ringing of a bell from the dispersal. When 'Mop' and I used to do this we read books, which was considered very eccentric and effete.

'Mop' was Pilot Officer Rank—Mop for his great bush of fair hair. He was something of a soulmate in philistine squadron life. I was reading Dos Passos and he was reading *Horizon* when the handbell clanged one afternoon, and up went the red light.

Magazine and book sailed through the air to the fire extinquisher airmen, crash went the Koffmans in unison, and without waiting to warm up we shot down the runway side by side. Mop had been reading Cyril Connolly with his helmet off because of the heat, and I was in convulsions behind my oxygen mask as I watched him struggle to do up the straps at the same time as withdrawing flaps, undercarriage and air intake, closing the hood and steering a compass course towards the foe.

We were given several vectors onto a supposed Hun with the Controller's voice reflecting his increasing excitement as the 'blips' moved about his radar screen. Thirty miles out to sea we broke through cloud into a clear patch, and there was our 'bandit'—a drifting barrage balloon.

'Bags I,' called out Mop.

'Like hell,' I responded briskly. We both went at it, eight

cannon against one bag of gas. There was a lovely woomph an a flash of flame and the remains dropped wanly into the grey North Sea.

'They counted as a kill in the Kaiser's War,' Mop remarked. 'Let's pretend it was a Dornier.'

Everybody was out again when we got back to Ludham, the broken muzzle caps on our guns proving that we had been in action.

'You lucky sod!' exclaimed Wimpey Jones as I climbed out onto the wing. 'Why do you get all the luck?'

'Nothing to it,' I said. 'It's only a matter of looking. Instinct, you could call it.'

I heard Mop say to a group of airmen, 'Went down in flames. Yes, we shared it. . . .'

Thank goodness, there was a lot of laughter during those first weeks in Norfolk that summer. When we were not on readiness we would scrounge transport and go out in the evenings, avoiding Norwich which was horribly blitzed and packed full of airmen, British, Commonwealth and American, all on the booze or after women.

There were some nice pubs where we could swim in the Broads and lie in the last of the sun. The farmers were hay-making and the corn was ripening for a bumper harvest. American Fortresses would limp back in broken formation from a daylight raid. Early in the morning we had watched them gaining height, immaculately tidy and hopeful of success then, their contrails scoreing the sky with white lines. Now their ordeal was over. Few of them, we could see, had four intact engines, and their numbers were much reduced.

Once I went a hundred miles out to guide and talk back one of these savagely mauled Fortresses, flying close alongside. There were gaping wounds in the fuselage and both pilots and several gunners were dead. The navigator was flying her on two engines and the bomber was steadily losing height. I guided him over the coast and gave a course to his airfield but had to leave him because I was running out of fuel. I waved and wished him luck but never discovered if he made it.

Mop and I bicycled about the lush countryside, talking about our families and the books we were reading. He loathed my hero Hemingway, just as Charlotte did, and we had fierce arguments. We visited Norfolk churches and twice went as far as Yarmouth which was like a town besieged, with fearful damage from tip-and-run raids and barbed wire and fortifications along the seafront. But a couple of cinemas were still open, full of our tormentors, the anti-aircraft gunners. The town was so quiet and the cinema walls so thin that I once impressed Mop by identifying Irene Dunne's voice from two streets away and before we even knew what was on. 'Now you see the benefit of being trained in Hollywood,' I remarked smugly.

The strain on the fitters of keeping enough Typhoons serviceable for ordinary operational demand proved too much and we became so short of aircraft that we were sent some old Hurricanes to keep our hands in at drogue firing and navigation exercises. I had to share my Georgina with Mop until the Gloster factory could make up our strength again.

In July we went over to the offensive and life became less carefree. It was half an hour across the North Sea to the Dutch coast and none of us felt entirely at ease at nought feet for 250 miles. Among the Sabre's less endearing habits was spilling oil back onto the windscreen, which at once made the sea, and everything else forward, invisible. The only solution was to slide open the window and very slowly and flatly ease your hand forward and round to the outside front of the screen to give it a single stroke with a rag. If you were to allow the slipstream to seize your hand, you would probably break your wrist. It was quite common at this time to see Typhoon pilots landing with their head sticking out sideways from the cockpit in order to see the ground.

We escorted and gave top cover to torpedo and rocket

Beaufighters which indulged in the suicidal practice of attacking convoys creeping along the Dutch coast. They were quite astonishingly brave, those Beau pilots, and we for once relished flak aimed at us because it gave them some sort of a chance of survival. Every convoy had at least one flak ship. These were, as the name suggests, a floating battery of anti-aircraft guns of all calibres. Sometimes the coastal guns joined in, too, and I remember looking back once as we started for home above the surviving Beaus and seeing the sky so thick with the drifting smoke from heavy flak that the coast was invisible.

We were supposed to protect them from the Schipol-based Focke-Wulfs and Messerschmitts, which seemed curiously shy when we were about. We tried to provoke them into action by flying inland and very low round the outer perimeter of Schipol. They could have outnumbered us ten to one if they had so chosen. But they still wouldn't come up and our scorn for the Hun daily increased.

Their flak was another problem altogether, and it began to take a nasty toll. First to go was an Australian, then poor Mop was blown up one morning early and I missed him very much. Two others disappeared over Holland a few days later.

Another Australian, with oil on his screen, miscalculated the height of the wave-tops at dawn and cartwheeled in far out to sea. When I got back to Ludham I went through the usual ritual of packing up his stuff, and noticed that the hut was emptying at the rate I had been told huts emptied in the R.F.C. during the Kaiser's War.

We drank more than usual in the mess that evening. But not as much as our lost Australian who turned up late and absolutely paralytic, having been miraculously picked up by a Yarmouth-based trawler and fed rum all the way home after being transferred to a Royal Navy motor torpedo boat. The next morning the only thing he was clear about was the shape of the sea bed out on some shallow bank. He had sunk only about five fathoms and claimed later that he had no trouble opening his hood, rising to the surface, inflating his dinghy and sunning himself until picked up half an hour later. Just then we needed that sort of encouragement.

With the tip-and-run menace judged to be finally finished, at the end of July we left Ludham for an even nicer airfield close to the village of Matlaske in north Norfolk. There we lived in style in an enormous hall with a lake in the grounds for swimming in the evenings. There were rumours that we were going to become even more offensive and lose entirely our role as fighters and become fighter-bombers or re-equip with rockets.

There was a very considerable esprit de corps in Fighter Command, especially since the Battle of Britain. We fancied our role as fighter pilots, liked leaving our top button undone and wearing silk scarves instead of collars and ties. Moreover, we regarded with some violence any weapon except guns as retrograde. Soon they'll make us drop hand grenades and darts like the R.F.C. pilots in 1914—that was our attitude to bombs and rockets.

But the truth was that there were fewer and fewer German fighters to fight: they were being sent to Russia or used to attack daylight bombers, and Bomber Command at night, too. And now, with the approach of the invasion of Europe, the Typhoon was to be switched to close support with the army and that meant bombs or rockets, and quick jabbing attacks against small targets at low level.

So, grumbling and swearing a great deal, we marked out a circle in the middle of Matlaske airfield and began to practice dive-bombing, using the gunsight for aiming. Unlike proper dive-bombers we had no air brakes and had to pull out at 1,500 feet or higher. It was very difficult to get anything at all into the circle, and the idea of hitting a moving tank appeared ludicrous.

Jonson muttered something about a live target—would anyone like a go? I said all right, I didn't mind.

'It's full moon tomorrow,' he added as if air warfare was now embracing astrology.

I was puzzled and asked about the moon's relevance. 'Oh, it's a night rhubarb.'

I gave a fair display of being unastonished and flew Georgina down to Manston in Kent where they screwed some racks under her wings and clipped a couple of 250-pounders to the racks.

To have under your control anything as lethal as a Typhoon complete with bombs and a full complement of high explosive shells; and to be given the duty of blowing up more or less what you liked, and be commended for doing so, was every destructive schoolboy's dream. From middle age I look back on these improbable and improbably named night rhubarbs with a certain degree of scepticism. Rushing about northern France and the Low Countries in the dark at low level, squirting away at trains and barges and airfields, disturbing a great many people's sleep, all seems a long way from E.E.C. and other present-day manifestations of the brotherhood of man.

But it is not such a distant memory as all that, and is on quite a different time scale beside those of our contemporaries who can well remember England when the good Queen was on the throne. Only a few years after the war I based the opening of my first boys' adventure novel on one of these rhubarbs. My hero got shot down—what else in a book called *The Perilous Descent*?—and I didn't, though on a number of occasions I should have been, including a foolhardy shoot-up of St Omer, the most heavily defended airfield in occupied France.

On these rhubarbs, searchlights sprouted up from the least expected places, including blue searchlights which blinded worse than yellow, and many a time tracer light flak made pretty dancing patterns around Georgina. Light flak at night seemed to come towards you at first even more lazily, its trajectory suggesting that it could never actually reach you; and then at the last moment the shells changed their mind as if supercharged and whooshed past at a million miles an hour.

The only answer was to leave as soon and as fast as possible. On my second trip at the next full moon and this time with delayed action 500-pounders, I got a lovely locomotive, one of those black French ones that always seemed pretentiously large and muscular for their duties. Then I used up all my shells on its wagons, which caught fire very satisfactorily.

I regret to say that squadron life, and the numerous efforts by German gunners to deprive me of it, had temporarily (see later) cast out any remaining doubts about the rights and wrongs of what I was doing. To knock a Messerschmitt or two into the sea at dusk, to shoot up a darkened factory, was a clinical operation which I viewed with a complete detachment from reality. I saw no corpse. I saw no blood.

I never actually relished blowing things up and killing people, but a blazing train on a moonlight night outside Lille scored the same satisfactory mark on my consciousness as a good try at school rugger.

As for my father, I was more than ever diffident about discussing what I was doing for fear of further confusing his doubt-ridden mind. He may have been pleased that I was 'doing my bit'—in that awful revived expression—but he was not going to let on. I think he also preferred keeping at bay any deep contemplation of my activities, which, after all, *were* very un-Shavian.

He and my mother came and stayed in Norfolk near me for a while that summer. It was not a great success. I was in a remote place and there was practically no public transport and nothing much for them to do but mooch about the lanes and sit in the sun. And they were both active people who lived for working to a routine in their house and garden.

Jonson's wife was staying in the same hotel. This led to a curious situation. Between us there was a marked seniority gap, although they had very kindly pushed me up a rank from Sergeant after my first kill. Jonson was a just but rather severe Flight Commander, and when we all had dinner together it might have been parents and child and headmaster and wife embarrassingly together at half term, mutually thrashing out some behavioural problem that had recently evidenced itself. I could almost hear Jonson saying, 'His climbing turns are showing better promise this term, but his dive bombing accuracy leaves much to be desired . . .' That sort of thing.

Actually, we didn't talk flying or the war even. Just staccato small talk while I nodded off over my coffee. Jonson had put me on early standby for three mornings in a row, which meant getting up at half-past three, in order to qualify for evening leave like this.

Afterwards, my mother said, 'You look peaky, dear.'

'Nothing that a good walk won't cure,' said my father. 'Too much drink and hanging about doing nothing,' he added with a laugh. Although the hotel was within the airfield's circuit and our Typhoons flew low over his head dozens of times a day, he never enquired what we were doing, although by any measure it was quite interesting. For example, that morning at five o'clock I had seen quite a lot of Holland inland from Egmond-Texel, witnessed a lot of flak including a heavy shell which had hit my number two, and—negatively but we had searched hard —attempted to find a convoy the Beau boys wanted to get at.

I think that there were two reasons for this odd state of affairs: first, he did not want my mother to be unnecessarily worried, and also he was anxious for himself to avoid moral discomfiture which accounts of destruction might arouse. He knew that I must have killed at least one man on my 21st birthday. But we never talked about that and there was a tacit understanding between us, which lasted for the rest of the war, that I should be silent or at least unspecific about what I was up to.

All this further widened the yawning gulf between our minds which grieved me greatly and bored us both horribly as, in a young man's selfish way, what I was doing totally consumed my consciousness and I did not have much else to talk about.

I came close to sleeping on my bicycle as I pedalled back to my hut that evening, and was still half asleep when I groped my way down to the dispersal again before dawn for immediate readiness.

My parents left early, ostensibly because my brother's harvest had begun and he needed them on his farm in Gloucestershire. But the relief all round was scarcely concealed.

Georgina went the way of most Typhoons, blown to pieces somewhere over Holland. I was sorry to see her go, and even sorrier to lose the friend who was flying her. Working my way through the alphabet, my new Tiffy was H for Harry. Almost from the beginning Typhoons had black and white stripes painted under their wings to distinguish them from the Focke-Wulf 190, which they resembled too closely for trigger-happy friendly pilots, and of course our ack-ack gunners, and the Royal Navy, too, who banged away at us happily and inaccurately whenever opportunity occurred, stripes or no stripes. Harry had a white-painted nose, for even clearer distinction, which looked very smart, but made no difference. American Thunderbolts and Mustangs were especially prone to blazing away at us.

Harry came with the autumn. There was no time to reflect on the summer until I went on rest in the winter when I could look back with full and mixed feelings—of fear and excitement and that special and exquisite experience of reversing the seemingly inevitable and lethal course of fate and being not only alive but uninjured.

Wimpey Jones, the happiest and funniest man on the squadron, had married the girl he had been in love with since he had been a boy, had returned glowing from honeymoon leave and been killed almost at once.

I had married, under similar circumstances, a few weeks later. I rented a little car from my father, scrounged some petrol, and Charlotte and I honeymooned in a hotel in the Lake District. It was full of middle-aged Army officers and their stiff middle-class wives who made clear their distaste for me, my service, my non-commissioned rank; and their jealousy of Charlotte (who looked agonisingly fetching in her W.R.N.S. uniform) and my car. For a week we climbed and ate bilberries in the sun and forgot the war and flying and everything else except the immediate second.

My commission coincided with the arrival of Harry. I walked out of Moss Bros, as hundreds did daily, all stiff and shiny in my new uniform, ashamed of my new-sproggishness when I fancied myself a veteran after almost a year on ops. I took the stiffening out of my hat and bashed it about and spilt things on it and generally encouraged it to get greasy.

195 moved again in September, this time to Fairlop in Essex, almost in the eastern suburbs of London. Charlotte was doing cypher work in the Admiralty. Somehow I contrived to keep the little car going—garages could be kind to pilots—and also contrived to pick up Charlotte in Trafalgar Square outside the Admiralty at all hours and take her back to the little cottage in Hertfordshire we now shared with her mother.

Once I finished a night rhubarb at 2 a.m., was refuelled and back at Fairlop at 3, and under the Admiralty Arch at 4 a.m. It was like a scene from one of those ghastly war pictures with Greer Garson as we drove home humming the latest Vera Lynn hit.

On 195 we got better at dive-bombing. Early in November we were briefed urgently on entirely new and mysterious targets —what appeared to be chalk white slits cut into the fields and woods of the Pas de Calais.

'These are Noball sites,' the Spy told us, and blushed at the raucous guffaws which greeted this statement. Somebody told him to pitch his voice higher and the C.O. shut him up.

'They are secret weapon sites of some description,' Spy continued gamely. 'We're not quite sure but we do know they are dangerous and are going to get top priority.'

This was my first brush with the doodlebug which was to figure importantly in my life, off and on, for the next fifteen months. We went down to Manston and for several days bombed with 3 Squadron whenever the weather allowed.

At first sight these ops looked like what we would call (and R.A.F. slang *was* incorrigible) 'a piece of cake'. The launching sites were only a few minutes' flying from the Kent coast and you could almost glide back with a dud engine. It was crisp and clear and at our operating height of 8,000 feet you could see far down the French and English coasts, the two landscapes with such similar colour and topography that you could slide them together in your mind like jigsaw pieces.

We kept in very loose formation, the two squadrons of twelve planes each half a mile apart. High above us some top cover Spits sparkled in turn as they weaved alertly from side to side. To see their protective presence was half a comfort, half an affront: we husky Typhoons nannied by mere Spits!

As it turned out, nothing came down on us. But plenty came up. None of us had seen flak like this before, even off the Dutch coast. In seconds the sky before and behind, above and below, and on both sides, was scored with black puffs. The shells exploded with a tiny intense yellow heart, faded fast from black to grey and drifted and dissolved astern, dirtying the blue of a perfect autumn day. We all jinked and skidded independently, rising and dropping a few hundred feet at a time until we were over the target.

There was no doubt that the Germans regarded these innocuous-looking strips as highly important. They could not be camouflaged and it was easy to pick them out. It was less easy to hit them, especially with all that hate crashing about you.

Taylor bawled out, 'Right, going down *now*,' and did so, showing his stripes and bombs as he flipped onto his back and set his Tiffy at 70 degrees. With an extra half-ton on board he fell away at a remarkable speed and was soon lost against the green of France. We were supposed to follow in regular succession. It looked safer down there than up here, and our haste to get onto our backs was indecent.

Before I went down I saw two holes in my starboard wing, and I saw one of 3 Squadron enter, but fail to emerge from, a yellow cloud of what I was later told was phosphorous flak.

Medium bomber Bostons had already been out here earlier in the day and the craters of their bombs peppered the fields around the white scar I had selected for myself. I squeezed my thumb when I was as low as I dared, and with a lot of light flak darting about now, and then pulled up so hard that I blacked out for several seconds.

The only thing in one's mind after bombing was getting out as fast as possible, with survival as the first priority. The aftermath of dive-bombing was rarely decorous. That morning we made very difficult targets even for those lethally skilful German flak gunners as we scattered about the sky, going flat out at all altitudes, but all heading finally for those friendly looking white cliffs of Dover.

3 Squadron was suffering rather badly just then. Lunch in their mess was a sober occasion, which turned moody when we were all told to swallow down our coffee as we were off again in half an hour. Poor old Harry was hit once more but showed no signs of minding.

Later in the month we moved along to Tangmere near Chichester to have a go at the Cherbourg peninsula sites. Everybody was attacking them now, the heavy bombers of Bomber Command (to 'Bomber' Harris's fury), the Americans, 2 Group as well as us. They had even slung a single bomb under the Spitfire. Casualties were heavy and at the time it appeared to be a very high price in lives, aircraft and high explosive for the doubtful benefit of getting a few bombs into narrow slits in the ground, an occupation as difficult as those maddening fairground competitions.

The last time I went out, and the last time I flew with 195, Harry was hit with great vigour, and on the way back over the Channel Isles, the Sabre conked out, recovered and conked out again.

In the ensuing silence I could hear the full chorus of the explosions about me as every gunner homed in on the likeliest victim they could see in the sky—straggler Hough.

Some kind Tiffy pilot fell back to give me company, and as a gesture of gratitude after we had lost a few thousand feet, the engine stuttered into action again. Fifteen minutes later I landed my beloved, scarred Harry from an operation for the last time.

After a year, to the day, on 195 I was posted away for a rest I felt I did not need. Several of us left at the same time, and we were all in a very disgruntled condition, expecting, at the worst, to be put onto drogue towing or sent to Training Command to become instructors.

Instead, a few days later, I was listening obediently to a dapper, middle-aged Group Captain.

'Your flying days are over, Hough, and you ought to be thankful,' he informed me crisply. 'You've had a good run and a bit of luck this last year so count your blessings. The war'll be over before your time's up. Good show!'

And it might have been my old friend of Bel Air with the pencil thin moustache.

195 Squadron and its Sabre-tooth Tiger badge with the motto 'Velocitate fortis' ('Strong by Speed'), had the shortest life of any Typhoon squadron. Everyone I had liked had been killed by the time I left; and I never met anyone from it again, except the only pilot who could not take it and had to be transferred to ground duties. I met him again on the day I was finally discharged in 1946. He was plumper and highly pleased with himself and his singularly elevated rank. I am confident that he has done well since.

In my mind 195 will always be associated with the hot hectic summer of 1943, the evocative countryside of Norfolk, and its wide open skies which, that year, seemed to echo day and night to the thunder of air warfare and the ripping-calico roar of the phenomenal Sabre.

6

It was worse than the Group Captain had threatened. The dread word controller was heard, and I thought in anguish, 'It can't be true, it *can't* be true!' That proud wizzo fighter pilot, Captain Ball, to radar controller, the lowest of low-bred penguin.

Pilots could be horribly snobbish sometimes, and in our eyes controllers combined the characteristics of the three monkeys who neither saw, spoke nor heard evil. They failed to observe fifteen raiding Messerschmitts, and then panicked. They sent you off on wrong vectors. They were dim ex-schoolmasters who sat in dark Nissen huts watching a white arm sweeping round and round a glass screen, flanked by unwashed W.A.A.F.s.

Drogue-towing, glider-towing, instructing—anything, I begged. The posting was confirmed. Hough to Woodlands Controllers' Training Unit, Bentley Priory, w.e.f. 14 January 1944. What had I done to deserve such a fate?

One huge consolation was that I would be within walking distance of Charlotte, now out of the W.R.N.S. and expecting our first child.

There was another consolation, too, and it lay in the bizarre nature of our life and activities in jolly Middlesex.

Bentley Priory had been the sacred headquarters of well-named Fighter Command during the Battle of Britain; although, now that the R.A.F. was more decisively on the offensive than ever before, some lunatic had re-named it Air Defence of Great Britain.

The large, ugly Edwardian mansion of Woodlands, just down the road from Bentley Priory, might well have been the headquarters of some fearfully hush-hush organisation engaged in the training of saboteurs for work in Occupied Europe—learning about high explosives in the conservatory, falling off the billiards table backwards for parachuting practice—that sort of thing. I am certain that the neighbours were more mystified by our activities as a Controllers' T.U. than if we had been a Saboteurs' T.U. The mere name 'controller' had a sinister ring—controlling what, pray, and *how*? All we lacked in our *dramatis personae* were Evelyn Waugh, Randolph Churchill and Graham Greene at his slinkiest.

The large drawing-room of Woodlands had been converted into a dummy ops room, clearly and gruesomely signposted Operations Room. Those uplifting R.A.F. films after the war were to familiarise the common people with what went on inside. In the space once occupied by chintz sofas, armchairs, brass-topped tables from Benares with elephant legs used for Mahjong, was an enormous mounted map of south-east England and north-east France and the Low Countries. Airfields, sectors and groups were properly marked out, and coloured counters with figures on them represented R.A.F. Squadrons and German Geschwaders.

Where once 'The Stag at Bay' had hung from the wall there was now a chinagraph board and another board showing the Order of Battle. Business-like but rather plain W.A.A.F.s in shirt sleeves with dark patches under their arms moved squadrons and wings about with sticks like garden hoes, or clambered boldly up ladders to attend to the boards. They wore headsets and the wires emanated from their ears like ectoplasm.

In the Minstrels' Gallery there sat, cool of demeanour, crisp and decisive of speech, the Head Controller himself, running an interminable dress rehearsal for some future super Battle of Britain. He was flanked by two trainee officers, who were sometimes allowed to scramble a squadron and intercept the hated Hun in mid-Channel.

All this made perfectly good sense. But in their zeal and their tireless search for authenticity, the founder of this school had gone one better. The Woodlands garden had been converted into an enlarged replica of the operations table in the drawing-room. Lurking motionless in the woods of Woodlands were more ex-fighter pilot radar trainees. Each was given the name of a well-known radar station like Poling, Beachy Head or Ventnor. They were also given a compass and an instrument like a surveyor's sighting stick to help track down the German Geschwaders when they came. Because the early weeks of 1944 were particularly wet, the laurels dripped mercilessly down the necks of these miserable radar stations.

On circles roughly marked out in white by a squeaky sports field line-marker, there lurked the Spitfire and Hurricane Squadrons of Fighter Command, props turning over, eager for combat and to be scrambled at a word from the Chief Controller within.

The squelchy lawn, which must once have witnessed so many closely fought games of croquet amid laughter late into summer evenings, was now the English Channel. Beyond it on foreign soil, bombed up and armed on their airfields, were the Luftwaffe's Kampfgeschwaders, the Stukageschwaders, and the Jagdgeschwaders.

Both foe and friend were represented by more trainee controllers. Unlike the wet stationary radar stations, theirs was a life of movement and action. Each pilot had an ex-Walls or Eldorado Ice Cream tricycle, fitted with real aircraft radio set where once lay the 4d tubs, 3d choc-ices and 2d bricks. Where once those friendly men in their smart peaked caps and white overalls would lift the lid to meet your order, there now was secured a proper Spitfire's compass and a proper London College of Music metronome with 150, 200, 250, 300 and so on marked on them to indicate everything from Adagio to Vivace.

In the cockpit sat the pilot, representing a dozen Spitfires or Messerschmitts, earphones clamped to his head, a microphone at the ready. He was instructed to ignore the Hun taking off, climbing and winging his way towards the white cliffs of Dover in his hundreds. 'After all, you can't see St Omer from Tangmere, can you?'

Not until the wet and forlorn radar stations spotted them could any action be taken. 'Bandits climbing over Cap Gris Nez, angels 12, steering two nine zero,' flashed the vital message to the ops room. A W.A.A.F. moved a counter with croupier-like speed. The Chief Controller called out, 'I have some trade for you', and scrambled a squadron from Manston. Out on the lawn a Walls stop-me-and-buy-one, its peacetime ownership still visible through the grey paint, lurched into motion. The squadron skidded slightly on the wet grass, setting course as instructed and setting the metronome at a Spitfire's best climbing speed which the pilot conformed to scrupulously with his pedal rotations.

The battle was stepped up as more Geschwaders took off and pedalled laboriously north—tick-tock, tick-tock on the metronome, the 'Horst Wessel Song' on the pilot's lips.

Soon the radar stations were flashing messages every few seconds and the English Channel became a veritable holocaust as Spitfires clashed with Messerschmitts and Hurricanes decimated the Stukas. 'Tally ho!' flashed across the ether time and again. 'This is Sentinel Red 3, Sentinel Red 3, have sent down 2 Bandits in flames—Over.'

Sometimes the holocaust became a wild anarchy. 'Like bloody hell you shot me down!' complained a Flight Lieutenant with a D.F.C. 'You haven't even sighted me yet, you Hun swine!' sounded out amid the rattle of machine-guns and cannon—'Rat-tat-tat—got you!'

It was three o'clock in the afternoon, drizzling lightly, we were full of Bentley Priory gin, fed up with placid pedalling. An Irish sergeant pilot who had been torn away from his real Mark IX Spitfire only three days earlier was now getting his own back. He had set his metronome at 1,500 mph and emerged from behind a rhododendron at a dizzy rate downhill. 'Out of ammo—ramming instead,' and he did so, striking a lumbering Dornier squadron head on and sending it into a turf-tearing skid.

'Achtung Spitfirer!' 'I guess I'm bailing out,' shouted a Canadian Warrant Officer with a D.F.M., and he rolled over into the grass, leaving his Spitfire to charge pilotless down a bank and deep into Hun territory.

In the Ops Room the W.A.A.F.s at first made an attempt to keep pace with the movements outside. They soon gave up. It was always the same in the afternoon sessions—'Well, really, I suppose they think they're clever. Silly babies, I call them.' And they took off their headsets and lit up ciggies from crumpled paper packets.

The Chief Controller sighed. Until this course he had had tame penguins, diligent and serious in their shiny new uniforms, straight from good class grammar schools. But what could you do with this mob?

The rain came down harder and pilots and radar stations alike streamed indoors, still loud with success claims. A solemn man gave us an elocution lesson instead. 'Say your Rs like this for c-l-a-r-i-t-y.' Sometimes he sat in a little sound-proof cabin with us in turn, taping our inelegant accents. Once he put his hand on the knee of a roughish Australian Beaufighter pilot. There was a noise beyond the decibel capacity of the recorder, and the solemn man retired hurt, as they say in cricket, and was not seen again.

Slowly, reluctantly, we learned the basic elements of watching a tube, recognising a blip, working out its speed and vectoring another blip to intercept it. It was not really very difficult but it was infinitely boring.

Still resentful and complaining, we were then scattered about the country to G.C.I. (for Ground Control Interception) stations. I found myself, improbably, first in the middle of nowhere in Bedfordshire, and then at a freezing Nissen hut in a place on the north-east coast called Seaton Snook. I was billeted out.

There was a crabbed and complaining doctor in his big, luxurious house who drank a double whisky before and a pint of Guinness with every meal and never offered me a drop. His conversation was exclusively of road accident injuries, described in lurid detail over the tapioca pudding, broken by complaints that he rarely got paid in full by the victim's family. In five weeks he never even knew my name.

By contrast, there was a warm-hearted bosomy Geordie lady, who polished and swept and cooked like a dream and adored her mountainous steelworker husband and always put me to bed with a hot water bottle.

Controllers, we learned, went on ops like pilots, and other controllers viewed you with respect if you had done a tour in the thick of it on the south-east coast. So when I was told that I would be going to the top of Beachy Head I was regarded with some awe, almost as if I had volunteered for some suicide mission.

They had an enormous piece of revolving wire netting on the top of Beachy Head called a T16, and it was regarded as very hush-hush, very low-seeing. It was presided over by a man called Bill Igoe. There was also a penguin Flight Lieutenant, another ex-pilot, and me. Also a pretty W.A.A.F. officer. (Women, being calmer, made better controllers than men. They never got in a flap.)

To the horror of the hotel proprietor, we drinkers and smokers were compulsorily billeted in a comfortable Plymouth Brethren hotel in Eastbourne. Like their forebears, they suffered bravely for many weeks. We even brought along our wives, who attracted doubtful glances.

'We're watching for the Hun secret weapon,' Igoe warned. 'You'll recognise it when it comes—very, very fast, dead straight course, no pilot, just a lot of T.N.T. Code word is "Diver".'

Had all that expensive bombing of the autumn and winter been a waste of time? I asked Igoe, remembering those friends I had seen go down in pieces and a few worried moments of my own.

Igoe told me that it had knocked out most of the permanent launching sites, but the Germans had extemporised a lightweight moveable platform which was almost impossible to spot in woodland clearings. When they came it would be in large numbers. First target: London.

One day when I went on early morning watch the Channel was one great white blip. It was the invasion going in on 6 June 1944. We watched for Luftwaffe intervention but saw nothing. I went out onto the cliffs and looked down Channel. It was a chill grey June day, inappropriate for the greatest military operation in history, and I could hear and see nothing. Perhaps the day the Normans had put their wet feet onto the beach a few miles in the opposite direction had been as unimpressive as this.

I was off watch when the first doodlebugs came in a few days later. There was an atmosphere of crisis in the dark, stuffy Nissen hut when I got there. 'You can almost see them taking off,' Igoe exclaimed. 'And, my God, they *go*!'

The next night, surprisingly, was silent. Then on 15 June, when I had been staring at that stupid tube for a mere hour or two, a smudge appeared a few miles inside France. It gained height with remarkable speed and I watched in consternation as the blips marched across the Channel with a great stride at every sweep.

'Nothing will ever catch that,' I pronounced, and picked up three more blips almost at once from more flying bombs. Mercifully, I was later to be proved absolutely wrong.

I vectored a section of Spitfires onto an interception course with a blip that was coming straight for Beachy Head. 'Diver, Diver!' I transmitted. 'Square 27, course. . . .'

I ran out of the controller's hut as it approached, and with two or three airmen and a collection of awed W.A.A.F.s heard for the first time the off-beat rattle of the doodlebug's primitive engine. It swept overhead with inflexible purposefulness, straight as a ruled line, devastating, implacable. Its stubby, squared-off wings and cigar-like fuselage were to become as familiar as its sound.

A Spitfire had made an intercept and was on its tail, but the distance between pursuer and pursued widened alarmingly even as the flying bomb raced overhead, and the pilot never got near enough to open fire.

The south-east England defences responded as swiftly as the fearsome crisis demanded. A balloon barrage was strung in a line south of London, General Pile's anti-aircraft guns were tactically re-sited to give them a chance of knocking the terror weapons out of the sky before they reached the capital, and we and Fairlight and other radar stations tightly co-ordinated our efforts to get the fighters onto them even before they reached the coast.

The Poles were the most enterprising. They resented not having any Germans to kill, but they rapidly worked up a passionate hatred for these science-fiction monsters. In their old Spitfires, straight and level, they had no chance of catching them. So they did standing patrols three thousand feet above their usual operating height and dived down at full throttle when they came in.

One or two of the Poles learned to save ammunition by getting their wing tip under the doodlebug's wing and in the few seconds while their speeds matched, tipping it over onto its back. They liked to do this almost over our heads, and then cackled with Polish laughter over the R/T as our precarious Nissen hut trembled from the ensuing explosion.

On a good, clear afternoon you might see the black puffs of half a dozen doodlebugs exploded in mid-air by cannon fire.

Twin-engine Mosquito fighters were brought into the battle, too, but until the advent of the Meteor jet, the only machine that was really fast enough was the Typhoon's new stablemate, the Tempest.

Roland Beamont became an ace doodlebug killer. He was a delight to control, instant in his responses, relying unquestioningly on your information and instructions until he got a 'visual', when he quite rightly cut you out of his consideration and instantly began on the business of destruction. Beamont perfected the art of shooting them down safely and quickly, and rapidly worked up a score of 32 destroyed.

When we had 'controlled' the destruction of 500 doodlebugs we gave Beamont and a number of other pilots a party at Bexhill. Five hundred 'kills' sounded impressive, but we were not doing well enough. Too many flying bombs were getting through, and there were just not enough really fast fighters to cope. The Germans had originally planned the onslaught on ten times this scale, and that would have made the later destruction of Dresden seem like a picnic and might well have ended the War in Germany's favour. So, as Igoe had indicated, the bombing of the sites had not indeed been a waste of time, which is something the intellectual anti-bomber historians of today should remember.

After a month of the attacks, I had to come up to London by train, and it was a heart-breaking experience. All the way from the outer suburbs, on both sides of the track, were the ugly scars of shattered houses—half a dozen or more destroyed and perhaps fifty damaged by each explosion. I remembered all those doodlebugs that had slipped through when I had been on watch and realised that we were losing the battle and had no business to be patting ourselves on the back with statistics of 'kills'. It was Londoners who were being killed.

We now know how badly shattered and near to breaking was London's morale at this time, and how preoccupied the Combined Chiefs of Staff and War Cabinet were. A decision was made to re-deploy all the defences, giving priority to the guns. General Pile had recently got American proximity fuses, the S.C.R. 584 and the B.T.L. Predictor. His gunners had hardly hit a thing up to now but that was because the guns were still not advantageously sited. So argued Pile, and he convinced Churchill that he could do wonders if he was given the coastal strip and as far out to sea as he could shoot.

We, on Beachy Head, were outraged. Our fighters were now restricted to the Channel or far inland. But Pile's was the right move. The first time I saw the battery behind Eastbourne in action I realised that, and knew that we might beat this terror weapon after all.

In cloud or clear weather, by day or by night, the guns picked off almost every doodlebug that came within their range, working up to a climax of 82%.

The noise of the guns and the exploding flying bombs was cacophonous, shell splinters battered the roofs of Eastbourne homes and the nearby fields were pitted with the craters of those that were not exploded in the sky. London still had much suffering to endure, from V1 and the rocket V2. But the worst was over. As the Allied armies forced their way east and over-ran the more westerly launching sites, our radar screens on Beachy Head were less stained by those streaking blips and the sky seen from the cliff tops appeared clear of the doom-laden sound and sight of the doodlebugs.

Controlling had had its moments, and perhaps the decision to make me, and others who had completed an ops tour, do a job which demanded a high degree of concentration was not after all so foolish as we had judged. It was certainly more productive than sitting about in a control tower or teaching the rudiments of flying to a new young generation.

It had been exciting as well as taxing to control, say, three Tempests, a Mosquito, a Mustang and a Spitfire, and bring them to a point of interception with six flying bombs simultaneously, allowing for the different speeds of the aircraft and the responses of the pilots. To guide a pilot onto a doodlebug in the few minutes this fast lethal weapon took to cross the Channel was a fascinating exercise.

But when there was nothing going on it was a dull, unrewarding occupation compared with squadron flying. Now, in September 1944, my radar screen was as empty as my future. The war was moving east with increasing momentum and I was still stinging from that Group Captain's patronising prediction nine months earlier.

So, late in the summer, around Arnhem time, I determined to prove him wrong. At Bentley Priory I had met a number of permanent headquarters staff of mainly lowly rank but of massive power, like certain grades of the civil service in peacetime who manipulate the course of destiny from drab Whitehall offices over chipped cups of tea. Because they were Fighter Command they left the top button of their jackets undone, and they wore silk scarves instead of ties and flying boots instead of shoes, although none had ever left the ground except for the little leap demanded at their medical.

These penguin Fighter Command men were the subject of mixed irritation and hilarity among visiting operational pilots, who always made a point of dressing rather formally at Bentley Priory, thus demonstrating their own snobbishness too. Most of these penguins had been doing the same job for four or five years and lived a complete peacetime existence with their wives in rented Stanmore houses and flats, their children at the local private schools.

I used to lose at billiards with one of these officers. He had the singular power of manipulating appointments. On a 48-hour leave I visited him in his office, was duly beaten by him at billiards, and then bought him a large gin at the bar.

'I want to get back onto flying, Chris.'

'Impossible,' he said, draining his glass and holding it up to the light to make sure none was left.

'Operational flying.'

'Don't be daft. Out of the question.'

I signalled the barman. 'Typhoons. But I would compromise with Tempests.'

Less critically now, Chris held up the glass again. 'Do you know,' he asked, 'there are *several thousand* fully trained pilots that Second T.A.F. can draw on. There are sergeant pilots cleaning out lavatories and eating out their hearts in transit camps from here to Montreal. There are . . .'

'Oh shut up,' I told him briskly. 'I have done well over a hundred hours on Spits and Hurricanes, a full twelve-month tour on Typhoons. I didn't need a rest, but now I've had it. And I know perfectly well that one telephone call from you can fix me a posting to one of the Second T.A.F. wings. Now.'

'They're all dropping bombs or rockets, you know.' He placed his empty glass less steadily on the bar counter. 'None of that rat-tat-tat I got a Messerschmitt stuff now.'

Chris looked at me with extreme gravity, loosening his silk scarf and swaying only slightly. 'It is against special orders issued by Lord Tr-Trenchard and W-W-Winston Churchill. But you'll have your posting in the fairly foreseeable future. And don't tell anyone, you bloody pest. . . . Ah, ta very much, perhaps I will.'

The thing was done in two stages. First I was given a stooge job because of my radar experience, flying about in Mark 11 Hurricanes and Mark 11 Spitfires exercising yet more trainee controllers by trying to make them lose me on their screen. I did not find this even faintly amusing but was thankful to be at the airborne end of the exercise rather than in their claustrophobic tin huts with that terrible sweep going round and round.

This was a mercifully brief stint, and very soon I was studying with the critical eye of a veteran bruiser my old antagonist. The Typhoon had been smoothed out since I had last known her. The quaint car door which had made getting in and out such a chore had been replaced by a one-piece sliding hood, a whip aerial replaced the stout mast, the propeller was four-bladed instead of three-bladed, and she was reputed to be marginally faster with the new series Sabre engine. And surely the Sabre must be a more reliable and less oil-spilling engine than it had been when I had suffered my first defeat in its hands two years earlier?

A handful of pilots were converting to Typhoons at Aston Down but I was allowed away without any preliminaries. Very nice, too, I thought. Worth every penny those double gins had cost me. I went up to 20,000 feet. It was clear and crisp, I could see most of the south of England from the Quantocks to the South Downs and the glinting Channel, and I felt drunk from the adrenalin-stirring sense of power the massive engine, the four projecting cannon and the primitive masculinity the Tiffy always induced in me.

I did a very slow roll, and as I sank out of it, losing at least two thousand feet, I was reminded again of the sheer weight of the beast. *Not* a suitable machine for reinstating my reputation over darling Ginger's head, I told myself, and wondered how those nice, funny, glittery, kindly and hospitable stars of golden kinemaland were getting on. Were, I shuddered, new spotty youths now flaunting their white bodies beside Kay Francis's pool?

'Rockets,' said the Wing Commander in the mess at lunch. It was an expletive. 'You'd better use 'em. You've always had bloody bombs, I know, but you may get rockets. They're not easy to hit with but they don't half tear up the Hun.'

All the world had seen what Typhoon rockets had done to German armour and transport in the Falaise Gap in the Normandy breakout. Four under each wing, and together they packed a bigger punch than the broadside of a cruiser.

I did not much care for them. The rails reduced your speed and affected the handling. It was difficult to get the right angle in the dive. I kept missing. The trouble, I found, lay in the fact that there was an immediate gravity drop. The only way to overcome this was by approaching the target vertically, and from a low altitude. The first was possible, the second was also possible but suicidal. I got a bit better and learned to turn sharply after releasing them in order to check their line by the eight trails of smoke they streamed behind them.

Late in 1944 my posting came through to Lasham in Hampshire, a sort of staging post for aircrew en route to 2nd T.A.F. on the Continent. Charlotte left the baby in London and came down for a last night at a hotel in Alton. It was only after I had left that I realised how nice it had been that she hadn't said anything emotional, and how stupidly slow I had been to recognise this. She knew what a struggle I had had to get off the ground again but never referred to it except, apparently, to share my delight when I won.

I was glad to go by sea and train and lorry. The journey from Calais and through Belgium evoked all that I had read about going up to the front again after a spot of leave in Blighty in the Kaiser War: the sudden stops and starts and long delays in crowded carriages and transit huts, the winter air steaming with the cold breath of tired troops stamping life back into their feet. The spirit of weary cynicism and fatalism must have been far more intense in 1918 than in 1945, but it was still there. Hadn't everyone said it was going to be all over three months ago?

The guns lit up the sky and shook the windows of the Nissen hut where I spent the night. Again, it might have been Ludendorff's last big push instead of the aftermath of von Runstedt's last great 1944 offensive which had been halted only a week or two earlier.

The next day I saw blasted trees, smashed villages, tanks rotting in the ditches, and all the characteristic debris left by fighting armies on the move. Antwerp was a ghastly sight: hollow-cheeked people, hollow buildings, the smell of death and hopelessness in the air. Black clad women with old scarves

133

round their heads picked for coke lumps on the railway tracks and ill men clanked by on tyre-less bicycles.

It was my first sight of what Germany had done to Europe. What it was doing to the city of Antwerp even now was horrible. From well-hidden sites in Holland, the enemy was pouring in doodlebugs and V2 rockets by the hundred, killing civilians by the thousand. Antwerp was receiving something nearer the weight and density of flying bomb attack that London would have had but for the bombing and the elaborate counter-attack laid on by the R.A.F. and the Army. Antwerp was getting almost none of this support. The defence of Belgian civilians had a low priority in the hurly-burly of a mobile war in its last stages. Antwerp was a tired, half-starved city, without civilian defence facilities, being pounded to death. Several more weeks were to pass before the flying bomb and V2 sites were overrun and the destruction ceased.

From the airfield in the suburbs to which I had been posted we watched the doodlebugs stutter overhead, cut out, and drop into the centre of the city with a shuddering crash. Half a minute might pass before the black cloud of dust and smoke rose into the sky. Another fifty dead.

197 Squadron was a tough, scarred Typhoon bomber squadron which, like 195, had been formed with early machines in November 1942. Its career and movements had been similar to my old squadron's up to the time of 195's disbandment in February 1944, and 197 had also converted to bombing in readiness for D-Day. My old C.O., Don Taylor, had commanded it at the time of the invasion, though no longer, and since then it had been engaged in all manner of close liaison bombing work with the advancing armies.

197 had lost a lot of planes and a few pilots on the way up from Normandy, and when I arrived the squadron struck me as being tired. It was almost without aircraft as it had suffered heavily a few days earlier when the Luftwaffe had engaged in a large scale and daring low level attack against many Allied

airfields, shrewdly timing it at hangover dawn on 1st January.

Some more Typhoons arrived soon after me, but a week passed before we got back onto operations again. We were living in the shells of suburban houses on the perimeter of the airfield, camping out under the less broken parts of the roof with the haunting fragments of an extinguished domestic life. A few pictures still clung to the walls, there was a sofa downstairs which told of quiet evenings with gossip, glasses of calvados and the bakelite wireless transmitting interminable accordion music. I found a child's sock in a near demolished chest of drawers.

Unlike the civilians, we were getting the food all right even if it was plain fare. But we were as badly equipped to deal with the cold as they were. We tore the remains of the houses to pieces around us to burn in the grates, and it was as well that we left when we did because the chest of drawers, the last sock and the last of the floorboards had gone up the chimney in flames.

Washing was too cold and elaborate a business. No one had washed for weeks, beyond a splash and a shave. We didn't undress at night. It was too cold. For flying, we pulled on lambswool jackets and dug out long unused inner gloves from the bottom of kitbags. But the Tiffy remained the warmest place.

It was a tough life after the soft semi-civilian existence I had been enjoying in England. But it was real military campaigning and I was glad I was there, and I am thankful that I did not miss the experience of seeing the last of the massive orthodox wars of history.

I liked most of the pilots, too. They were either of my vintage, or a little later, and 197 was typically international with a Belgian, a Siamese, several Australians, a pair of inseparable Rhodesian identical twins, some Irish. All the pilots had steeled themselves for a few more weeks of fighting, none believing that the war would last longer than that. Like any bunch of young men who have fought together for a long time under arduous circumstances, there was a complete understanding, and certainly nothing as amateur as line-shooting. Many months had passed since the last of the weaker, less enthusiastic pilots had been sent home; and those who had died in Normandy and during the long haul across Europe were already as distant a memory as, for me, were the pilots I had known on 195 who had been killed.

But the war lasted for months, not weeks, and it was a busy time for 197 right until the surrender in May. If some branches of the German war machine weakened during these last months, their flak did not. The German powers of accuracy, speed and sheer volume with their anti-aircraft fire did not diminish by one perceptible degree. We lost a lot of machines, and some pilots, although several of those shot down found their way back to us before the end of the war as the Army liberated prisoner of war camps.

The Typhoon was always game and versatile; you had to concede it that, whatever you might choose to say about its reliability. I had flown it first with a 100-pound, then a 250-pound bomb under each wing two summers before, and it had not minded at all. We thought that two 500-pounders was pushing our luck a bit, but I found out that, if you couldn't find your target you could save the R.A.F. money by landing back with the bombs, though you were not supposed to, and the wings never fell off. I had flown the Tiffy with cylindrical long-range tanks which almost doubled the range, and of course with eight rockets.

My faith in the strength of the Typhoon was limitless. But I was taken aback when I was ordered off with seven others from Antwerp with two 1,000-pounders, which was the bomb load of a proper twin-engined bomber not so long before. The C.O. observed my raised eyebrows. 'It's O.K.,' he said. 'Just takes longer to pull her off the ground, that's all.' Typically Tiffy.

136

We went up north on interdiction business. When the Army didn't need us we broke as many railway lines, bridges and roads as we could drop bombs on. We didn't always hit, but the bombing was much better, and also much steeper, than it had been on 195; and the 1,000-pounder was by fighter-bomber standards a real blockbuster.

That morning we went after a railway bridge just south of Leiden. There was not very much flak, the bridge quite disappeared, and we all got back unharmed—although I damaged an eardrum permanently as a result of dropping 7,000 feet with a catarrhal cold.

'Piece of cake,' everyone said; and after a year off ops I wondered again at the unchanging quality of R.A.F. slang. 'Wizard prang!' said Bob Gibbings, a nice farmer's boy, over some lunchtime beer in a cold tent. 'Good show,' said the C.O.

We smashed a few more bridges before we left Antwerp. It was pleasantly clean work which killed few if any people, except flak gunners sometimes. Our hatred of them was so far past any humanitarian consideration that, when opportunity occurred, we would risk our own necks for the opportunity of blowing them to pieces with cannon fire. This was done, after dropping and before pulling out of the dive, by kicking the rudder, sighting and very quickly getting in a burst at a flak gun site.

Early on the morning of 8 February we moved up in support of the Canadians who had opened a heavy offensive in the Reichswald forest and were having a difficult time. Again it might have been 1918 instead of 1945. The landscape looked just like Passchendaele, and the splintered trees and countless shell holes, the zig-zag of never-ending trenches, the long columns of lorries snaking up towards the front line, the sparkle of the guns from the east, created a repeat performance of those dreadful weeks in 1918.

Then, 'Watch for the Hun in the sun'—that's what Captain Ball always warned his men. And, even now, I did look up from time to time, but more from habit than from fear of being bounced. Unlike 1918 there were very few Huns left, and those that were had very little petrol.

Eight of us went down with anti-personnel cluster bombs west of the remains of Cleves, and followed the bombing with a low run along the Waffen S.S. trenches. They did not like this, and everybody was firing at us with anything they could lay their hands on—I thought I even saw one officer banging away with a Mauser pistol.

We did the same thing twice more that day, and my left leg began aching again from the effort of sliding the Tiffy from side to side at low level to distract the gunners.

'Wizard show!' said Bobby Farmiloe as we stumped into the Flight tent. I didn't think so really as I counted the holes. But if this sort of thing *had* to be done at all, it was best done in this chunk of flying steel. At Aston Down I had heard of a Tiffy which had survived quite happily when one ricocheting dummy rocket from the machine behind had gone through the port wing, and a second through the starboard wing.

We were at a place called Mill in Holland. Those nippy specialists who could create an airstrip in the middle of a swampy jungle almost overnight had carved a single runway out of the edge of a pine forest and even put up some wooden huts with stoves. The mud was real Flanders muck, but we had little else to grumble about.

On the first night in the mess I spied a much decorated Group Captain whose face was familiar. Our Group Captain? At the bar I studied him more closely and then plucked up courage and said, 'Do you remember, you directed me to my first California breakfast, sir?'

It was Johnny Baldwin, a fair, short, tough pilot who had managed to race through all the final training and get into a squadron long before I did, even allowing for my lost weeks in hospital. He had also been in right at the beginning of the tip-and-run business when the Typhoon first began to surprise and cut to pieces the Focke-Wulf 190. He had a good score, a

138

D.S.O. and D.F.C. and was very genial—a real Captain Ball. Baldwin led the wing sometimes, and always with tremendous panache. He was a relentless bomber, pulling out lower than anyone else would dare to go. He stayed on in the R.A.F. and was killed in the Korean war.

I liked the Belgian boy, Philippe. His was one of the few families to get out ahead of the German advance in 1940 and reach England. He had joined the R.A.F. as soon as he was old enough and had been with the squadron for nearly a year.

On dud days we got together a bridge four and crouched round the hut stove for hours on end, playing for a hundred mythical pounds a hundred. Sometimes we borrowed a jeep and explored the countryside and villages. There was nothing much to see, and nothing in those shops which had survived the German retreat. But we made friends with several local farmers who invited us into their pathetically bare polished houses and gave us terrible ersatz coffee. Their stern Dutch faces broke into beautiful smiles when we slipped them some sugar from the mess, and they struggled politely for the privilege of washing our clothes in exchange for half a bar of soap.

In the last months of the war, the new age of military technology began to impress itself on our simple life of crudely sending bombs down in exchange for shellfire coming up. Occasional German jet fighters darted overhead on reconnaissance. They looked completely uncatchable, and we now know that if Hitler had not done his usual meddling and interrupted production, they would have been an acute embarrassment. But by chance one day two nearby Tempests returning from an operation spotted a Messerschmitt 262 as it raced down the length of our runway very low. To our astonishment they caught it with comparative ease right before our eyes and sent it into the forest. Even more astonishing, the pilot survived. He turned out to be very young and green.

And then, by late February, thick cloud was no longer a deterrent to us dive bombers. Some scientist, who became very unpopular with us, had invented a form of blind bombing, straight and level, by radar. We felt very stupid flying in loose formation above 10/10th cloud and in blazing sun all pressing the bomb tit together when the distant voice over the R/T ordered us to do so.

We were told the bombing was highly accurate. 'If we're going to have a wizard prang, I like to see it,' someone complained.

We shrugged our veteran shoulders and talked gloomily of the imminent end of the pukka fighter pilot who judged by eye and instinct and flew by his ass.

We started some bright fires during those February and March days, blew up an ammunition train ('Hope it was f——ing flak ammo,' our new C.O. remarked.), cut a lot of railway lines, blew up barges and did a lot more 'cab rank' work for the Army just behind the German lines.

Three or four of 197 were shot down, including sturdy Bob Gibbings, who was back in 36 hours—surely one of the nippiest escapes of both world wars. Like all of us at this time he was wearing khaki uniform without wings or insignia. The Germans did not care for R.A.F. pilots, and we were also close to the Russians, who might confuse our R.A.F. uniform with Wehrmacht blue. To underline further our friendly relations with Joe Stalin and to prove we were not Huns we carried little silk Union Jacks with 'Ya Anglichahnin' (I am an Englishman) sewn into the centre.

On the night of 23 March some of us went up to join the gunners on the banks of the Rhine, the last of the really big obstacles left before the invasion of Germany. At dawn the infantry and paratroops would be going in. The barrage of rockets and shells against the German defending troops seemed to light the whole world bright yellow, and the ground pulsated with explosions.

I had flown for so many weeks over the corpses of the Arnhem and Nijmegen gliders, tilted and tattered among the

INSTRUCTIONS

(1) Learn by heart the Russian phrase "Ya Anglichánin" (means "I am English" and is *pronounced as spelt*).

(2) Carry this folder and contents in left breast pocket.

(3) If you have time before contact with Russian troops, take out the folder and attach it (*flag side outwards*) to front of pocket.

(4) When spotted by Russian troops put up your hands holding the flag in one of them and call out the phrase "Ya Anglichánin."

(5) If you are spotted before taking action as at para 3 do NOT attempt to extract folder or flag. Put up your hands and call out phrase "Ya Anglichánin". The folder will be found when you are searched.

(6) You must understand that these recognition aids CANNOT be accepted by Soviet troops as proof of bona fides as they may be copied by the

Я англичанин

"Ya Anglicháhnin" (*Pronounced as spelt*)

Пожалуйста   сообщите   Please communicate

shell holes from that desperate September battle, that I had forgotten what gliders looked like in the air, or even that they flew at all. But on the morning of 24 March, the air above the Rhine crossings was to be more densely populated than at any time in the Battle of Britain or even in the carrier battles of the Pacific.

Our briefing was short and to the point. 'Free-for-all today. It'll be a bloody shambles and they can't even find a code name for what we've got to do.' Our new C.O., Harding, sat on the floor of the hut with oily maps spread about him. He squashed out his cigarette on a board and lit another, using it as a pointer to our target area. 'About there,' he said, and took a thoughtful drag.

Ramrods, Lagoons, Jim Crows, Roadsteads, Rhubarbs—I had done them all. I could remember only one or two in which I had entirely escaped flak, and always we had been severely instructed to avoid going back to have a go at the gunners. These wretched assassins made you so angry that the temptation was sometimes irresistible; it was also nearly always fatal to have a second go.

'What have we got to do?'

'We've got to keep down the flak. It's going to have a riot with all those Dakotas and gliders and heaven knows what else. Every Tiffy in 2nd T.A.F. is going for flak posts this morning, and that's our area, there.' And he pointed again.

'It's all freelance. When you see the muzzle flash go down and give it hell. 500-pound anti-personnels, take-off in half an hour.'

The squadron was, for once, up to full strength and we had twelve serviceable aircraft. I went out to mine and gave her the usual look-over. In 197 only the C.O. and Flight Commanders had their own planes. The rest of us usually grabbed any machine, though we had our favourites. I knew this one all right. It had only a few patches from small flak repairs and the engine didn't spill much oil. I asked the rigger to give the

142

screen a wipe all the same. It was not going to be a good day for reduced visibility.

I sat on the wing, legs dangling between the protruding cannon, and lit a cigarette. The armourers were mucking about with the two fat bombs under the wings. Two of them were talking luridly about the Dutch girls they had taken out the night before.

We knew all the erks by name and our relationship with them was entirely democratic. An operational squadron living out in the rough as we had done for so long was closer to the supposed ideal of an egalitarian society than any left wing politician could aspire to—relaxed in style, laconic in communication.

One of them pulled himself up by the gun barrels and took a light from the end of my cigarette. Within a few feet of us in my plane were thousands of rounds of high explosive shell, a thousand pounds of anti-personnel bombs and two hundred or so gallons of high octane fuel. Back at Coltishall we should both have been court-martialled.

'They're doing the f——ing Rhine today, eh?'

'That's right. Quite a party.'

'You're doing the trenches, are you, with these APs?'

'Gunposts, Jim. And it's time to go.' We stubbed our fags out on the wing and he slid off and ran to a passing bomb trolley, jumping on board to save the walk.

Three hardstandings away the C.O.'s prop was already turning and he was shouting at Red Mason who was late at his aircraft and still lumbering out with his 'chute banging against his buttocks.

The Mustangs which shared our strip had already gone. They were to meet the gliders and give them fighter escort. One of them had just come back early, in trouble, and had flipped upside down on landing with unpleasant results. About a hundred erks had run out and cleared the wreckage away for us.

We taxied out quickly and took off in pairs into a clear sky,

143

formed up briefly and then broke up again as we neared our operating area. There was no difficulty in finding it. The night-long bombardment, and the fires it had started, had filled the air with slow-drifting smoke which combined with the early morning mist near to the river to make visibility very poor.

I dropped down low over the fields to the east of the Rhine, wondering how the glider trains would manage in these conditions. But I suddenly saw that some of them were already arriving, wallowing aerial armadas that seemed to fill the sky.

Already to port and starboard, above and below, released gliders were floating nose well down, fast towards their landing areas. Some were being fired at and badly hit. One right under me turned over on touch down and spilt out everyone.

On my port side a Dakota plummeted out of control and on fire and went into a wood. It was impossible to tell if the parachutes were the crew or paratroops who were falling by plan in small scattered groups from other Dakotas.

I weaved about at my favourite height of 50 to 250 feet, fussed because I couldn't find a flak post while all this damage was being done and so many were dying. The Germans were master camouflagers and there was so much drifting smoke and mist that I began to feel helpless and as if trapped in some frustrated dream sequence. Above all I was angry.

Another Tiffy crossed in front of my nose. I caught a glimpse of the 197 leters OV on his side and noted that his bombs had gone. I turned sharp to starboard in the direction he had come from and saw a glint of muzzle flash among some trees. 20 mm. tracer like a fireman's hose came up from a four-gun automatic battery, and I could just make out some figures moving among the trees and between barrels of heavy flak guns that were crashing away as hard as they could go.

I don't suppose that the short burst I gave them with my guns had much effect, but it had genuine feeling behind it and I was able to drop my two big APs in the area before skidding and skating my way out as fast as I could go. The flak didn't follow me. If they had any guns left they were after juicier targets.

The kaleidoscope of falling planes and men, gliders landing seemingly without plan if they were not shot out of the sky first, of smoke of every shade and hue, and sometimes the sharp blaze of flame from building or machine, all seen from the solitariness of a fighter's cockpit, left me stunned and anguished. It seemed that the Rhine crossing was ending up as a terrible shambles, even more terrible than that at Arnhem six months earlier, and with appalling casualties.

After another half hour of dodging about through the clouds of smoke, avoiding the Dakotas and gliders that were still pouring in, I shot off the rest of my ammunition at what I thought was a German gun post, and then pulled up and out of the maelstrom.

Everyone else's impressions were similar, and it was difficult to make any clear report on the results. Here, and no mistake, we had seen 'the blood-red blossom of war with a heart of fire'. And I thought I had witnessed, too, a terrible Allied defeat. But we were all wrong. As we ate a scratch lunch down at the Flight in the warm Spring weather we were told that the British and American armies were across and well entrenched, with few casualties, and were already linking up with the air-borne divisions.

The telephone rang in the squadron office and the C.O. came out a few minutes later. 'Come on, chaps, we're wanted for tank-busting now. . . .'

The war in Europe still had six weeks to run. Neither in the air nor on the ground did it fade out in that time. The Wehrmacht contested every yard of German soil, and, it seemed, with increasing fanaticism as younger and younger and more ardent Hitler Jugend troops were brought up to the front line, full of Vaterland doctrine and skilful with their weapons.

We were ordered out to a number of villages held by these

suicide boys. They could be taken only at very high cost on the ground. We bombed and bombed again places like Winnekendonk until there was nothing left—and nobody left except a handful of stunned boys who could hardly walk with their hands above their heads.

In those last hectic weeks we bombed guns and tanks and airfields and ships, straffed barns reputedly full of S.S., destroyed a camouflaged telephone exchange outside Utrecht, even dropped surrender leaflets.

My number two and I scouted around the coast with long range tanks picking up the occasional truck, and once, gloriously, setting fire to a store of jerrycans as high as a house. Anything that moved on the roads was fair game as only the military had petrol. But sometimes military traffic mixed in with the refugees in their horse-drawn vehicles. I saw open trucks crammed with infantry with innocent oxen- and horse-drawn carts in front and behind. Of course we killed civilians—we couldn't help it.

Least pleasant of all was shooting up individual cars and trucks—they looked so jaunty, vulnerable and innocent speeding along the straight roads. So four years of war had not, after all, snuffed out those un-Captain Ball boyhood guilts and doubts. Did the degree of guilt depend on how much you saw of the destruction you meted out? I think it did, and you sometimes saw too much when ground straffing.

At the same time, with the hunter's instinct, the heart lifted with excitement at the sight of a target below and the hunter's blood ran faster as you pushed down the stick, opened the throttle wide, made a quick intercept calculation, switched on the sight and slipped the shield from the gun button.

On 7 April, on the second of two long trips, three of us picked up some trucks near Groningen and I gave the other two top cover against any of the German fighters which sometimes still roamed about, while they went down. After Hartley and I dealt with a staff car a few minutes later, the other two gave me cover when I spotted another staff car going fast along a tree-lined road.

I was going over 400 mph in the dive and I opened fire a second too early. As I pulled up the nose a fraction I could see the cannon strikes dancing along the road like an hysterically fast fuse racing to its point of detonation.

The car was packed with passengers—there must have been five or six people inside, and not one with the sense to keep a look-out through a window. My glimpse of them, alive, intact perhaps talking together and smoking, was one frame from a film, flickering like the Odessa steps sequence from Eisenstein's *Potemkin*. The next frame, as the full weight of my shells tore in, was all blood and fire.

Before I was over the top of the blazing ball I felt a violent thud and the Tiffy tried to turn right over. As powerful and immediate as my panic-stricken response was the age-old sense of guilt and just retribution. If I had died then, as I knew I was about to die, and deserved to die, I would have died with peace in my heart and with my brain registering that justice had indeed been done.

The certainty of death was overwhelming. But my strength must have remained undiminished, for I did not quite strike the ground as had seemed inevitable. I succeeded in hauling the machine onto a more even keel and climbed away, searching the sky for more of the flak that, by incredible chance, had sprung from some concealed post on that lonely road. There was none. But I saw that my tail was in a terrible state.

The other two came down to join me. 'What the hell have you done to yourself?' Hartley called out.

'Flak.'

He moved in closer and studied my tail in detail. 'You *are* in a mess, aren't you? One of your wheels is down, too. And what's happened to your hood?'

I told him I had ejected it because I thought I was going to have to get out in a hurry. They hugged me comfortingly on each side for the long, arm-aching trip back to base. It was also a very cold trip, at 200 mph at 8,000 feet without a hood and with a rather uncertain airframe.

Back at Mill I flew low and slow past the control tower while Baldwin examined my poor old Tiffy through binoculars. A belly landing was all right, and two locked wheels was all right even in my damaged condition. But one wheel had *not* locked, it was wobbling about, and a one-wheel landing in a Tiffy with half a tail and no flaps was an uncomfortable prospect.

'Do you want to bail out?' Baldwin asked.

'No.'

'Go to Volkel and put her down on the grass, then. I'll send somebody for you. Good luck.'

I wondered whether the 'somebody' was to be a surgeon or just a driver to drive me home. Volkel was the nearby Tempest airstrip with some nice grass useful for crash landings. Emergencies on metal link strips, which were the basis of temporary runways, led to sparks and sometimes to fire.

The crash wagon and ambulance were ominously waiting when I came in, fast and unstable at 130 mph, trying to touch down on my starboard and tail wheels only without putting my starboard wing into the ground. It worked quite well, and when I had to put a little weight on the loose port wheel it even held up for a time before it keeled over, sending my Tiffy into a series of ground spins, dirt and clods of grass flying everywhere. But it did not throw me onto my back, for which I was very grateful.

The ambulance crew were trying to lift me out before I had undone my straps. Then we all ran fifty yards, waiting for the fire that never came. I was quite unhurt and my shivering was caused by the prolonged freezing cold of that open cockpit. But the first draw on the cigarette was more glorious than ever, and I was also given a stiff brandy before being packed off back to Mill.

Later, when I looked more carefully at the wreck, I reckoned that some at least of the tail damage was caused by the ejected hood. Had my very sharp pullout above that doomed car broken my port wheel lock, which at that speed would have thrown me onto my back? Perhaps there had been no flak and my near catastrophe had been brought about by some supernatural power of retribution? In my thankfulness I was prepared to believe anything.

I did another dozen or more ops after this. But somehow the spirit of aggression had died with those people in the car. I went out early the next morning on the same sort of roving mission and we did a lot of damage to transport of various kinds around Wilhelmshaven. The flak was atrocious and I was hit badly.

When I got back there was a letter from Charlotte with some photographs of our baby—fair curly hair, smiling on the lawn among the toys of her first birthday. I got excessively drunk that evening and realised that my nerves were not quite as good as they had been.

The next day was rough, too. The C.O. and I, with two more covering us, systematically dismembered an enormously long train and blew up its locomotive, staining the sky of north Germany with the smoke. After this we did some more straffing along the roads. The flak was worse than ever and the other two were soon shot down.

With Germany dying on her feet it seemed a stupid time to get killed. Almost overnight, the Captain Ball figure began to falter, and then to fade. Charlotte's mother, with a year-old child, had lost her first husband like this, in 1918, when the shooting was almost over. The next day one of the Rhodesian twins was blown to pieces bombing a ship off Bremershaven. I never heard his brother speak again.

I found myself walking less briskly to briefings, and by no means in the front row when pairs or fours were selected for straffing ops. Late in April I did two hectic bombing and straffing trips on villages in one afternoon and returned to find a leave signal—a flimsy bit of paper that was also a passport to survival.

I think I realised then that I had fired my last round, dropped my last bomb and picked up my last flak fragments. That afternoon I took off as a passenger in a leave Dakota for England.

The fuselage of the old warhorse was packed with stores, old blankets, and with jubilant airmen below the rank of corporal. It was all very jolly, and as the only officer, and with a well-trained eye on the main chance, I was as quick as anyone at finding a cosy corner in which to stretch out. I lay on a pile of blankets, my head on a kitbag, reading and dreaming—dreaming rather soppily of the better half standing in the cottage porch beneath the scented honeysuckle, a little child—my child—in her arms, an embroidered handkerchief fluttering a welcome. Ah, what a warrior's homecoming!

It was bumpy over the Low Countries, and soon I began to feel less well disposed towards the world. Then by merry, almost melodramatic chance, the news of Germany's surrender came over the radio to the Dakota exactly as we winged our way over the white cliffs of Dover.

The radio operator put his head out of the cabin door and yelled, 'It's f——ing over,' and slammed it again. The erks went mad, rushing up and down and starting a kitbag fight. The Dakota lurched about worse than ever under the impact of falling bodies and kitbags.

'Oh God,' I thought. 'What ghastly humiliation! Here am I, the one fighter pilot on board, two tours behind me, the pride of Ronald Colman. And now a disgrace to the King's uniform and commission.' My mind went back with sickening dizziness to that awful boyhood crossing of the North Sea, and the *Louis Pasteur*, and my instructor throwing me about in the goddam Stearman. Oh. . . .

'Come on, sir, the war's over—aren't you glad?' The airman

began to pull me to my feet before he noticed the pallor of my complexion. 'Sorry, sir,'—and he returned to the fray with gusto.

I shut my eyes, swallowed painfully, and lay very still.